WE WERE BROTHERS

Center Point
Large Print

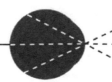

**This Large Print Book carries the
Seal of Approval of N.A.V.H.**

WE WERE BROTHERS

Barry Moser

CENTER POINT LARGE PRINT
THORNDIKE, MAINE

This Center Point Large Print edition
is published in the year 2015 by arrangement with
Algonquin Books of Chapel Hill,
a division of Workman Publishing.

The text of this Large Print edition is unabridged.
In other aspects, this book may vary from the original edition.
Printed in the United States of America on permanent paper.
Set in 16-point Times New Roman type.

ISBN: 978-1-62899-754-5

Library of Congress Cataloging-in-Publication Data

Moser, Barry, author.
We were brothers : a memoir / Barry Moser.
pages (large print) cm
Summary: "Illustrator Barry Moser renders the memories of his youth—
in luminous drawings and candid prose—on his quest to understand how
he and his identically raised brother could have become such very different
men"—Provided by publisher.
Reprint of: Chapel Hill, North Carolina : Algonquin Books of
Chapel Hill, 2015.
ISBN 978-1-62899-754-5 (library binding : alk. paper)
1. Moser, Barry—Childhood and youth. 2. Moser, Barry—Family.
3. Illustrators—United States—Biography.
4. Moser, Tommy, 1937–2005.
5. Brothers—United States—Biography. 6. Difference (Psychology)
7. Alienation (Social psychology) 8. Reconciliation.
9. Chattanooga Region (Tenn.)—Biography.
10. Chattanooga Region (Tenn.)—Race relations—History—20th century.
I. Title.
NC975.5.M68A2 2015b
741.6092—dc23
[B]
2015028530

WE WERE
BROTHERS

Barry and Tommy Moser, c. 1943

PROLOGUE

I HAVE A FAMILY photograph that was taken on a Christmas Eve sometime in the early 1960s. We are in my aunt's living room. Two generations pose in front of a fireplace that, as far as I know, never entertained an actual fire. Above the garlanded mantel hangs a portrait of my aunt's late husband that I painted when I was in high school. The people in the picture are my mother's people: her husband, sisters, and brother are there, as well as my brother and me. Most of us lived cheek to jowl on a short stretch of a Chattanooga country road.

All the people in the picture are dead now—Mother, Daddy, aunts, uncles, cousins, and my brother, Tommy. I am the only one still alive.

Since my brother died I have reflected on our relationship, mostly in the context of that country road and those people in the picture—Haggards, Holmeses, Coxes, Moores, Mosers. And I have reflected on the culture that shaped them and shaped my brother and me. Without opportunity to be otherwise, Tommy and I were racists, born into the byzantine machinations of the Jim Crow South. Tommy in 1937. I in 1940.

As we grew up Tommy and I went our separate ways. He stayed in the South. I moved to New

England. And for nearly forty years the distance between us widened and at one point it seemed that the gulf had become so vast it would never be bridged and we would be forever strangers. We both hardened, but I hardened more than he.

Though when I read novels and stories or see films in which brothers are close and go places together and have adventures, I often weep. I weep even when they fight, as they do in Jim Harrison's splendid novella *Legends of the Fall*, because in the end blood and love win out over the divisiveness that once separated the brothers. Or the contentious, yet deeply affectionate relationship between Norman Maclean and his estranged brother, Paul, in *A River Runs Through It*, or between Alvin and Lyle Straight in the *The Straight Story*. The childhood miseries of Frank and Malachy McCourt in *Angela's Ashes* moved me profoundly because they were shared miseries between the brothers.

In Abraham Verghese's transcendent *Cutting for Stone*, Shiva Stone, a surgeon, says that "life is in the end about fixing holes." Though Shiva speaks about surgical holes, his twin brother, Marion Stone, who is also a surgeon, takes it as a metaphor for another kind of hole, "and that is the hole that divides a family." What he owes his brother most is "to tell the story. . . . Only the telling can heal the rift that separates my brother and me," he says. "Yes, I have infinite faith in the craft of surgery, but no surgeon can heal the kind of wound that divides two brothers. Where silk and steel fail, story must succeed."

OUR FATHER, ARTHUR BOYD MOSER, had no siblings. However our daddy (our stepfather), Chesher Holmes, had four brothers, all younger than he and all of whom lived in Chattanooga or within easy driving distance. The few times we saw his brothers were at breakfast on Christmas Day at their mother's place on the western slope of Missionary Ridge. That was our only connection. None of his brothers ever set foot in our house on Shallowford Road. Daddy told me once that he had raised his four brothers, his daughter, and my brother and me—and that may very well be the case, certainly the last part of it is. But the thing is, Daddy didn't much talk about his brothers. Oh, he told stories about his brother David, who had a goat cart as a boy, and about his brother Martin, who was an extra in a war movie that starred Victor Mature, but that's about all.

He didn't fish or hunt with his brothers, nor did he socialize with them. As a family, we visited his youngest brother, Gene, at his home when he was recuperating from a motorcycle accident in which he lost one of his legs. We visited his brother Dan and his wife, Beverly, at his mother's house after Beverly had given birth to a new baby. And I have a vague memory of visiting with his brother

David after he returned from the European Theater in World War II. He gave Daddy a 9mm Mauser rifle that he brought home as a war trophy.

My brother and I were never privy to any personal interactions between the Holmes brothers other than on those Christmas mornings when they bantered among themselves while they posed for photographs with their aging mother. All of them smiling broadly, presenting the face of a congenial family. And maybe they were, who knows? But there were never any displays of affection. There was no playful roughhousing of the sort that would make affection seem to be part of the fabric of their relationship.

On the other hand my brother and I were not privy to any discord, if there was any, among the Holmes brothers. To us they were a world apart. Five entities who went about their individual lives, unconnected to and seemingly unconcerned with each other.

It was like that with my uncle Bob, too. He had two brothers, but he spent his weekends fishing with Daddy rather than hanging out with his kin. Like Daddy, he saw them on special occasions: their mother's and father's birthdays, Christmas, New Year's Day.

I know more about my grandfather, Albert Moser, and his relationship with his two brothers, Will and George, than I do of any of the other brotherhoods in my family. From a 1932 letter

George Moser wrote to his nephew, my father, I know that those brothers fought, that they went to hog auctions together, that they loved dogs, that they harbored deep resentments about the outcome of the Civil War and the subsequent Reconstruction. And I know that George greatly admired his older brother, Albert.

But the only brotherhood I have any firsthand knowledge of is my own, and, for the most part, it was heavy ladened and knotty. Like all siblings, we vied for the attention of our elders. We both wanted to be the favorite son. We both wanted to have the most friends or to be one specific friend's best friend. When I see the genuine and gentle interactions between my four nephews, I respond with gladness—and tears. I envy them that. Prodigously.

Though our personalities were like oil and water, I loved my brother and he loved me. It just took too long for us to understand it. To admit it. And to try to do something about it. The blame for our conflicts does not lie at my brother's feet alone because I certainly contributed to the strife that so nettled our relationship. But I am the teller of this story, or at least I am the teller of *this* version of this story, and I can only see it through *my* eyes. I can recall it only through *my* memories, and thus I have the advantage.

In the end, I rue the fact that during our life-times my brother, Thomas LaFayette Moser, and I rarely experienced deeply affectionate moments like those real and fictive that I have observed and read about. Only near the end of his life—and after forty years of living a thousand miles apart, both geographically and emotionally, a distance that was punctuated by rare visits and infrequent phone calls—did the rancor genuinely abate. We were both in our sixties.

What follows is the story of that brotherhood. But to tell you the story of that brotherhood, I have to tell, as well as my abilities will allow, the story of our family, and of the neighborhood we lived in.

PART ONE
SHALLOWFORD

The thing is, all memory is fiction. You have to remember that. Of course, there are things that actually, certifiably happened, things where you can pinpoint the day, the hour, and the minute. When you think about it, though, those things mostly seem to happen to other people.

ROBERT GOOLRICK
Heading Out to Wonderful

Wilhelmina and Arthur Moser, c. 1935

SHALLOWFORD ROAD

SHALLOWFORD ROAD ORIGINATES at the western foot of Missionary Ridge, the scene of a fierce and bloody battle in the Civil War, part of the greater Battle of Chattanooga. The road ascends steeply, northward up the side where it crowns the brow of the ridge, and then gently descends the eastern slope until it levels out and meanders out into the country. My brother, Tommy, and I grew up in a small five-room house on Shallowford Road just after it levels out at the eastern foot of the ridge. Number 509. It was a white bungalow, the most popular style for houses built in America between 1930 and 1940. It had a low-pitched gable roof and an unenclosed porch supported on the corners by square, tapered columns that sat on masonry pedestals. This style of architecture originated in southern California and gained popularity nationally because the houses were so practical and easy to build. Bungalows became so popular that a customer could mail-order one and have it shipped and assembled on site. It was said that a bungalow could be built by anyone who could swing a hammer.

Arthur Boyd Moser, our father, bought the house for my mother, as best I can figure, from a family named Childers sometime around 1930. If that is so, it may have been a wedding present for Mother since she and Arthur Boyd married on November 11, 1930. It was right next door to the house belonging to Mother's brother, Floyd Haggard, and his wife, Grace. Mother's sister, Velma, and her husband, Bob, lived next door to Floyd and Grace, one house farther up the street toward the ridge. All our houses faced onto Shallowford Road, and from all our front porches we saw the same landscape on the other side of the street: a steep clay bank the color of tumeric, the result of the road being cut out of a hillside; the hill from which the road was cut, which was covered with dun-colored grass; and two houses at the top of the hill. The last time I drove by in 2009, it was all overgrown. There is no longer any evidence of the tumeric-colored bank, the grassy field, or either of the two houses that stood on the high ground.

My father made a lot of money. I have an incongruous photograph of him wearing a shirt and bow tie with STANDARD OIL embroidered above the breast pocket. He has a change maker hanging from his belt. But a man doesn't make the kind of money Arthur Boyd made, nor live as well as he did, by pumping gas. No. He made his money illegally. He shot craps in basements in Chattanooga, a rough and tumble town in those days. Even when I was a boy, the city had one of the highest crime rates in the nation, a manifestation, I was told, of making illegal corn whiskey. Ironically, it also boasted one of the highest per capita ratios of churches.

He drove around town in a big black Buick convertible. Mother said that it was the only car in Chattanooga with a radio in it. I don't know whether that was true or not. When he had a particularly good night at the local tables he'd come home and wake up Mother and off they'd go to Chicago to shoot craps in speakeasies in the Windy City. Mother told stories about the mobsters she ran into and the machine guns she saw up in the balconies of the Chicago gambling joints.

Arthur Boyd was a large man. He stood well over six feet tall and weighed about three hundred pounds. Mother didn't even come up to his shoulder. There were no clothes in an ordinary haberdashery to fit him, so he had them made by a black tailor named Napoleon "Nap" Turner. From the photographs I have of my father, he mostly favored light-colored suits and matching ties, fedoras, and shoes. Arthur Boyd (most everybody called him by both his given names) was an easygoing man who rarely lost his temper, though when he did, Mother told me, he threw skillets and broke furniture. But he never hit her.

I was told that I took after him in looks and personality. I wouldn't know since I never knew him, but I am an easygoing man who happens to have a god-awful temper. Like Arthur Boyd's, it rarely goes off, but when it does, I tend to break things, too.

Tommy on the other hand took after the Haggard side of the family, resembling our irascible uncle, Floyd Haggard, more than he did Arthur Boyd. Floyd was a tall man, handsome, who favored dark suits. He had a beautiful smile (when he smiled) but his temper was quick and often violent. He nearly killed a friend of his once for throwing him a peach.

"Hey, Floyd, catch!"

Floyd turned and caught it, not knowing what it was.

He had such a loathing of the texture of an unwashed peach that he recoiled even at the *thought* of touching one. He nearly beat his friend to death because the man knew about this aversion and hoodwinked him into catching it anyway.

ARTHUR BOYD'S GAMBLING DAYS ended when he was thirty years old. He developed brain cancer and died on August 1, 1941. He had been hospitalized in Grady Memorial Hospital in Atlanta for several months, during which time he lost most of his cognitive functions to the tumors that were swelling inside his head. He could count only to ten, and when he got to ten he went back to one again. And again. And again. Despite everything, he always recognized Mother's footsteps when she came walking down the hall toward his room. His face lit up and he smiled, Mother told us.

I was ten months old when Arthur Boyd died. Tommy was just about to turn three. Years later Tommy told me that he had a few memories of the man and his car, but they were very hazy.

When Arthur Boyd died, Mother's luxurious life came to an abrupt end. Just as the cancers had ravaged his brain, they also ravaged his accumulated wealth. In the early days of her youthful widowhood, all Mother had were the gifts he had given her—the bungalow, an engagement ring that was a full carat diamond in a platinum setting, a few furs, a car, two baby boys, and his Social Security.

It was a long way down for her.

Before she and Arthur Boyd moved into their pretty little house they lived in a comfortable apartment downtown where Mother had a black maid who reported to work in a gray-and-white uniform and answered to Mother's silver bell. I never heard that woman's name, or if I did, I don't remember it.

Even though the bungalow was paid for, there was hardly any money for upkeep and maintenance, so the property declined. Rats moved into the basement, and since there was no money for exterminators or pest control, they thrived. Not even a dozen of the large Victor rattraps were up to the killing job. When Tommy was older he did all he could to keep the house painted, the hedges trimmed, and the lawn manicured, but the lack of money inevitably showed, so while we were growing up it became an ordinary little house and Mother became familiar with a mortgage—eventually two of them. Had it not been for Mother's childhood friend Verneta, I am not sure she could have coped.

VERNETA

VERNETA WAS A BLACK WOMAN. Mother called her a "nigress" (accent on the first syllable, which rhymes with *fig*) when she had to call her by something other than her name. She lived in the large green-and-white farmhouse at the top of the hill across the street from us. It was very rare for black and white families in the South at that time to live that close together. Rarer still when the black folks' houses were on the higher ground. Be that as it may, there was always a pleasant harmony between our families because, as my mother often said, we all knew our places, both black and white. Knew and respected them.

Verneta helped take care of Tommy and me after Arthur Boyd died, but not in any formal capacity as a nanny or a maid. She did make her living as a domestic, but she took care of us boys because she loved Mother and was Mother's closest friend. Tommy and I both adored Verneta.

She and Mother grew up together in the 1910s and 1920s, a scant fifty years after Appomattox. These were the days of forced segregation when black and white children could not learn together, worship together, or eat or drink together in any public place, but they could run barefoot together in the summertime and play and laugh and become lifelong friends, as these two little girls did.

One of the places they played together was in the family grocery store.

Will Haggard, Mother's father, owned and ran the store until he died in 1931. Her sister Velma took over and was running the store when Tommy and I were little boys. It had a wide front porch and double screen doors with metal push plates declaring that COLONIAL BREAD IS GOOD BREAD. All that remains of that store today is a slab of concrete at the corner of Shallowford Road and Rockway Drive.

The porch was where men gathered to sit on benches and drink Cokes and swap stories. It was dark inside the store, especially when you came in from bright sunlight. Up front, near the screen doors, was a candy case that had a lot of nose prints on the glass that Tommy and I left. Behind the candy case were two wooden counters. An ornate brass cash register sat atop one, a small roll of brown wrapping paper on the other.

The interior walls were shelved from the uneven wooden floor to the stamped-metal ceiling. They were full of provisions that needed no refrigeration: Krispy saltine crackers; Ovaltine; jams and preserves; cans of coffee, fruits, and vegetables; PET Milk; patent medicines; and cartons of cigarettes. Green pendant lamps hung from the ceiling in two evenly spaced rows. There

Will Haggard's grocery store, c. 1930

were small windows up near the ceiling that let in a little light that was often hazy from Velma's cigarettes.

Farther toward the back of the store was a refrigerated case where fresh cuts of meat, wieners, cheese, and eggs were kept. Sticky yellow flypaper hung here and there, each one blackdotted with its emerald-eyed victims.

Behind the meat case was a walk-in cooler. Sides of beef and pork hung inside as well as a few bins for produce that needed or benefited from refrigeration, watermelons in particular.

Next to the cooler was a storage room. It had a single double-hung window that looked west across a hay field toward Missionary Ridge. A light bulb hung from the ceiling by an electrical wire that was tied off in a bowline knot and looked for all the world like a hangman's noose. You turned the light on by pulling a cord that had a bus token tied to the end of it. This was where Will Haggard kept his bulk stores: cracker barrels, flour barrels, salt.

One day in 1918 or 1919, my mother, who was always called Billie, and little Verneta were playing together at the store as they often did. Mother's older sisters, Velma and Annie Lee, came slapping in through those two big screen doors and announced that they were going downtown to see a moving picture show. They wanted to know if little Billie wanted to come along.

Well, of course little Billie wanted to go along—and so did little Verneta. They both got all excited about it, and in my imagination I see them jumping up and down and squealing. But then one of the older girls reminded Verneta that she couldn't go. I can hear Annie Lee saying something like,

"V'nita, don't you go bein' silly now. You know you caint go. Why, you know better than to even ask."

Verneta commenced to cry. But then, with a sudden jolt of inspiration, she ran to the back storage room. She pulled the cord and turned on the light. She threw the lid off the flour barrel, climbed up on a chair, bent over as far as she could, and stuck her little face into the flour. Then she ran back out to the front of the store and took Billie by the hand. The white dust made her little black eyes seem all that much blacker. I see motes of flour in the air and a trail of it on the floor. And I hear her hopeful question,

"Now can I go? Now can I go?"

It would have been like my mother to put her arms around Verneta and to try to wipe away the caked-on tears when she was told, once again, no, she couldn't go. Would have been like my mother to hold her friend and console her, because even though both of them had been taught what their proper and correct places were, it didn't mean that they couldn't love and comfort each other, as Verneta loved and comforted my mother when Arthur Boyd died and she helped take care of Billie's two baby boys.

AS I SAID, Tommy and I adored Verneta. She was in our lives nearly every day. She changed our diapers and made sugar tits for us to suck on. She took us to the park, and up the side of Lookout Mountain on the Incline, one of the steepest incline railroads in the world. But even so, Tommy and I grew up deeply racist. Why, I wonder, with such a woman in our early lives, a woman we spoke well of, and for whom we had deep affections, did we feel the way we did toward black people? Three black families, all kin to Verneta, lived right across the street from us, and no harm ever came to anybody in our family or theirs. There was never an unpleasant confrontation of any kind. There was no enmity. No animosity. Nevertheless, Tommy and I were taught that black folks were not—check, make that *never*—as good as we were. Not even the black dentist who lived in a fine stone house on the West Brow of Missionary Ridge that overlooked the city.

One day I was visiting Velma when she and a friend were drinking coffee in Velma's spacious kitchen. I was sitting at the table, too, just listening. They were talking about that dentist and I heard Velma say,

Verneta Gholston, c. 1955

"Law, I'd never let that nigger put his hands in *my* mouth."

"Hmmph. He could buy and sell you, Velma."

"I don't give a damn. I still wouldn't let him put his fingers in my mouth."

"Yeah, but you let niggers cook for you."

"Well, that's what they're supposed to do."

"Your sister lets one of 'em take care of her babies."

"That's different."

"How's it different?"

"It just is."

This was the sort of exchange that we grew up hearing from our family and from friends of our family. "Nigress" was the kindest word I ever heard applied to a black woman, and that only came from Mother when she referred to Verneta. Occasionally I would hear the more polite term, "colored," but more common was "coon," or "jigaboo." I don't think I heard the word "Negro," pronounced properly, until I was in high school. I certainly never used the word, nor did anybody else in our family. I remember one time referring to a black woman as a "lady," it could have been Verneta, and was soundly rebuked.

"There aint no such thing as a *nigger* lady, Barry. Don't ever forget that."

The word *nigger* was used as casually as the word *butter* in our family. Brazil nuts were "nigger toes." Black-eyed Susans were "nigger heads." A hard storm rained "cats, dogs, and little nigger babies."

Despite this environment, Tommy and I were brought up to respect, even like, an individual black person. But as far as our family was concerned the black *race* was slow, shiftless, and ignorant.

Very *smart* individual black folks were an exception. They were relegated to a place of out-of-the-ordinary loathing: Booker T. Washington. George Washington Carver. Ralph Abernathy. We had never heard of Paul Laurence Dunbar or W. E. B. Du Bois, but if we had, they, too, would have been dismissed as uppity niggers who thought they were as good as white folks. Paul Robeson and Marian Anderson held special places of contempt in the Shallowford pantheon of negrophobia as did Jackie Robinson and Nat King Cole.

I walked in on Velma one time while she was watching TV. She and Bob had the first TV set on our block and she was watching some program where Nat King Cole was singing. She was standing, wringing her hands when I walked in. When she saw me she said,

"Law, honey, you caint even turn the tee-vee on anymore without there being some black nigger on it."

I thought she was going to have a stroke when she spied a black family looking at a house that was for sale across the street from her backyard. Why that bothered her, and having Verneta and her family across the street in the other direction didn't, I don't know. Familiarity, perhaps. Or maybe because the Gholstons' houses were farther away. But all she could say standing there peeking through the curtains was,

"What am I gonna do? Law, law, what am I gonna do?"

MOST BLACK MUSICIANS, however, escaped our white reproval: Fats Waller and Jelly Roll Morton were particular favorites, as were the Ink Spots, Cab Calloway, Scott Joplin, Duke Ellington, and our fellow Chattanoogan, Bessie Smith.

We approved of the movie actor Stepin Fetchit because he was shiftless, slow-witted, and knew how and when to hold his hat in his hand. That's the way we liked our black men. He knew his place—on the screen. And my family liked him. A lot. Had they known how wealthy and influential he was offscreen they would have hated him, too.

As I look back with the perspective of a much older man, I see that my family's loathing was not strictly reserved for black folks. All of us were sensitive (perhaps overly so) to percieved slights from strangers who we assumed thought that they were better than we were. Or who, indeed, did enjoy a higher social status. We assumed that they looked down their noses at us—as we looked down on the white folks who lived near us who were not as prosperous as we were. My brother carried that chip of inferiority on his shoulder most of his life. And struggle with it as I may, I sometimes find myself in restaurants and other public places sizing up strangers with those old senses of base inferiority and outward enmity.

Chesher Holmes, c. 1950

CHESHER

MOTHER REMARRIED ON May 5, 1943, to Chesher Holmes. Tommy was five. I was two.

Chesher was a popular man in Chattanooga, especially in the sporting community. He was commodore of a couple of boating clubs on Lake Chickamauga, he refereed football and softball games, he judged diving competitions, and he organized youth basketball in Chattanooga in the 1950s. Even though he couldn't swim himself, he taught Tommy and me how to. He had a weekly radio show on WAGC called *The Sportsman's Hour*, where he interviewed people about hunting & fishing, guns & lures, and boats & motors. He mostly broadcast from a sound booth on the top floor of the Hotel Patten that stood at the corner of Ninth Street (now Martin Luther King Avenue) and Georgia Avenue. We sat and watched from the other side of the big glass window and were always tickled with delight when he told his listening audience that his two sons were with him in the studio that night.

Occasionally he did his broadcast from a federal courtroom on the second floor of the post office building with a live audience. Tommy and I loved going with him on *Sportsman's Hour* nights; we enjoyed the show but mostly loved going because we stopped for ice cream or milk shakes on the way home.

Chesher was a superb horseman, especially at jumping and playing polo. Tommy and I saw all his (mostly blue) ribbons one time at his mother's house. We were there for the usual Christmas breakfast, and she brought out the large box full of ribbons for us to admire. If he had not been diabetic he would have been a cavalryman in the U.S. Army. Since he couldn't join up he became an instructor of horsemanship for the Sixth Cavalry stationed at Fort Oglethorpe, Georgia, near the Chickamauga battlefields.

He and Mother met horseback riding in the woods on a Sunday morning. Chesher was a real sweet-talking charmer, so Mother invited him to come home with her for some breakfast and to meet her two little boys. According to Chesher, he accepted the invitation, came for biscuits and gravy, and never left.

When he came to live with us in our little house he came alone. He brought nothing with him other than his clothes and his horse, Tony.

Chesher became Daddy, the only Daddy we ever knew. He was good to Tommy and me. I think that he was afraid of being seen as the stereotypical mean stepfather, and thus he never struck either of us, other than the rare paddling with a harmless hairbrush. When he got really angry, he had a peculiar way of looking above and just to the right of our heads, avoiding direct eye contact. I asked him one time why he did that and he said that if he ever did look us in the eye when he was mad at us, he'd probably smack us.

Daddy took us to the movies. He took us to the Golden Gloves. He took us to see the Harlem Globetrotters when they came to Memorial Auditorium and played the black team from Howard High School. He took us fishing and taught us how to handle a rod and reel and how to pilot several kinds of boats, from flat-bottomed trolling boats to inboard cruisers and high-performance speedboats. He took us to the baseball games when the Chattanooga Lookouts played at home. He took us to softball games under the summer lights at Warner Park—women's slow-pitch and men's fast-pitch. He took us to the sulky races at the county fair, after which we climbed the steps to the top of the motordrome and watched motorcycles race up and around the cylindrical "Wall of Death." He walked with us down the midway, holding our hands, as we gawked at the sideshows and listened to the barkers hawking their goods. On Sundays he took us on long boat rides down the Tennessee River or on long car rides down the length of Lookout Mountain.

One Sunday afternoon we took Daddy's Chris-Craft runabout through the locks of Chickamauga Dam and rode all the way down to Williams

Island, about fifteen miles downriver. Tommy was at the wheel when we passed an upriver cruiser that was throwing a heavy wake. Tommy crossed the wake at such an angle that we were momen-tarily airborne, and when we slammed down hard, I swallowed my wad of chewing tobacco. It wasn't long before we turned around and headed back because I was sick. Daddy and Tommy were laughing their asses off as we passed the cruiser and left it in our wake. I haven't chewed tobacco since.

Another summer Sunday we were in Daddy's car, a four-door 1948 Chevrolet Stylemaster, headed out in the general direction of Lake Chickamauga, taking a route we often took, though we were headed nowhere in particular. Tommy and I had been fighting, as usual, and when he thought he couldn't be seen, he'd hit me. Not hard. Just aggravating me, was all. I hit him back because I knew that if Tommy got seriously mad at me and started hitting me really hard, Mother or Daddy was there to stop it before it got out of hand and I got hurt. We were still pestering each other when we turned off onto Lightfoot Mill Road, a little-used road that for a short way ran between Chickamauga Creek and a fertilizer plant that gave off a smell that registered somewhere between being oddly pleasant and sweetly nauseating. I had come down with a bad case of the hiccups right after we left home and Daddy was getting irritated with me, or so it seemed. We were right there between the creek and the fertilizer plant when he suddenly stopped the car. He got out, came around to my side, opened my door, and made me get out. He got back in and drove away. I could hear Mother yelling at him to stop. Tommy was yelling at him, too, I could tell, because I could see his anxious face mashed against the chrome-trimmed rear window.

Standing on the side of the hot road, smelling the repugnant odor of fertilizer, I started screaming and jumping up and down. One of my Buster Browns was untied and flew off. Tears were rolling down my dusty face. I yelled at the top of my little voice,

"Daddy! Don't leave me! Don't leave me! Please! PLEASE DADDY!"

He hadn't gone ten yards when he stopped the car, kicking up a cloud of dust and gravel. He opened his door, ran back to me with a big smile on his face, picked me up, hugged me tight, and asked,

"Where'd your hiccups go, li'l buddy?"

They were gone.

Daddy kissed me—smooched me, actually—several times, put me down, and opened the back door. I snuffled my way back up onto the backseat behind Mother. Tommy wouldn't look at me. He was crying. Daddy picked up my shoe and put it on my foot before he closed the door and drove on.

SUNNYSIDE

TOMMY WAS DIAGNOSED with amblyopia long before he started school. It is a common condition and causes more childhood blindness than all other causes combined. Tommy's specific ailment was strabismic amblyopia. His left eye turned in toward his nose. When that happens the vision becomes blurry and the brain shuts down that eye. Simply put, Tommy didn't see well. Nor did he do well in school. His bad eyesight predisposed him to being academically challenged, particularly when it came to reading. He had done so poorly in his first year in school that he was made to repeat the first grade at Eastdale Elementary School, which was about half a mile from our house up toward Hoyt Street. He repeated first grade, passed, and went on into the second grade.

When he finished the second grade, the local Board of Education redistricted the school system and Tommy had to change schools. His new school, Sunnyside Elementary, was a mile from our house in the opposite direction. But they did not accept his second-grade credentials from Eastdale Elementary, so he had to repeat the second grade, too.

This made him two years older than his

classmates, which put him in an unavoidable and socially awkward position, one that invited ridicule. He hated being called "crosseyes." Or "dummy." Or "moron." From that point on, Tommy was hypersensitive to failures, humiliations, slights, and hurts—both real and perceived. It didn't help that our aunts, uncles, and Daddy were always kidding him about his little brother.

"Better watch out, Tommy. Barry's gonna catch up with you one of these days. You better be careful."

I never corrected them. Never took Tommy's side.

One day Mother got a call from the principal, Mrs. Wright, a Virginian who pronounced *out* and *about* oddly. The semester had just begun. I would start school the next fall, so I was home with Mother when the call came. Tommy had been too embarrassed to ask for permission to go to the bathroom to do a "number two," so he held it. And he held it. Until finally he couldn't hold it any longer and just let it go. And he did. In his pants.

Mother borrowed a car from Velma, put me in the front seat (there were no laws against that in 1945, nor were there any such things as seat belts), and we drove to the school to get Tommy. He was standing out on the sidewalk with Mrs. Wright. He was crying. She was holding his hand. When he got in the backseat, Mother told him not to sit down because Velma had told her that

Tommy and Barry modeling football helmets for a
newspaper article about the new plastic helmets
that their daddy was selling, c. 1950

she didn't want any shit getting on her upholstery. So he stood up all the time. And all the time he kept whimpering, more or less in my ear,

"It's just a itty bit, Mamma, it's just a itty bit."

WHEN I STARTED SCHOOL in the fall of 1946, I went to Sunnyside, too. I was there from the first grade through the sixth. I did not go to kindergarten as Tommy had.

Sunnyside's main building was what, generously speaking, might be called Classic Revival, though not much of it was classic, except perhaps the odors associated with elementary schools of the time: glue, disinfectant, cafeteria, and the readily recognized, though hard to identify, odor of, well, elementary schools. It was a masonry building, with nine-over-one windows that peeled lead paint. The main structure was built during the 1920s or 1930s, and during the 1940s an addition was built to accommodate a new auditorium and a few new classrooms for the three lower grades.

I hated school just like Tommy did. It's impossible to say who hated school more, but I hated it, shall I say, *ardently*—and that may be an understatement. Like my brother, I didn't read well, though for different reasons. I was dyslexic. Or so I think I was, looking back. I was never diagnosed, even though the condition had been known since 1881. I'm not sure that *anybody* had been diagnosed with dyslexia in 1946 America. It really doesn't matter. What matters is that I was inept at memorizing poems or Bible verses. I had trouble conjugating verbs correctly, or reciting my times tables accurately, especially if I had to do it out loud. Both Tommy and I were utterly incompetent at playing the little red-and-white plastic recorder called a flutophone.

There were very few activities, curricular or extracurricular, that either of us liked—other than leaving school and going home.

Unless looking at *National Geographic* counts as an extracurricular activity. They were shelved, strangely enough, in the hallway outside Mrs. Wright's office, and I sat on the floor, sometimes with a friend or two, looking at them. When we were lucky, we found pictures of brown-skinned women with naked breasts, which always prompted little-boy giggles of embarrassment and titilation.

I had my fair share of insults to my young self-esteem, the same as Tommy. In the classroom some of my classmates called me "idiot" and "imbecile" under their breath because of my inability to memorize state capitals and the parts of speech. On the playground I was called "fatso" and "lard ass" and "slowpoke," because I was a fat kid and couldn't run very fast.

I didn't enjoy recess very much because I didn't have many playground skills. I was always the last boy to be chosen for the softball team because

I was slow and I couldn't hit the ball. And I had absolutely no sense of strategy. I was at my best when pretending to be a horse for the girls. And for this I was called "mama's boy" and "sissy." They giddyapped me all over their side of the playground with imaginary reins and bits. I could swing and seesaw pretty well, too, especially when I was swinging and seesawing with the girls. It seems that I have always enjoyed the company of women over the company of men.

If the temperature outside dipped below forty degrees, we had to stay indoors at recess and after lunch when normally we would be outside playing. As I think on this now, having lived through forty-eight cold New England winters, I wonder if the forty-degree rule might have had something to do with the kids who lived in the Chandliss Home, an orphanage that was across the street from Sunnyside. Perhaps they didn't have clothes that were warm enough to withstand even a moderate forty degrees.

SUNNYSIDE DIDN'T HAVE an art room, so when we had our rare art lessons we worked at our everyday desks. I might have looked forward to school more had there been art or craft lessons every day—or even once a week—but there weren't. Our curriculum was typical of the time— the three Rs, as our teachers called it: Readin', Ritin', and 'Rithmetic. Art and music were nonessential frills to the overall program, much like Bible lessons—though I am sure that our Bible lessons were considered far more important than our art lessons. This was the South, after all, where religion is like summer humidity (if you will allow a Faulknerian allusion)—you just can't get away from it, as hard as you might try.

No matter what grade we were in, we used the same uninspiring materials in our art lessons: colored construction paper, scissors, glue, poster paints, cheap brushes, and crayons. Despite the mundane materials, this is where I was first told that I had a talent for drawing. I don't really believe that I drew any better than any of the other kids, and I certainly did not draw better than Tommy. I just drew things that were more "realistic" than my classmates, and my teachers, thinking that a gift for verisimilitude was synonymous with artistic talent, patted me on the back. It was rare that I ever got academic pats on the back, so those occasional approbations felt good. And it's worth mentioning that I was fortunate that I never had a teacher "correct" my drawings. No one ever told me that I had drawn something wrong—as if any child could ever draw anything wrong.

I may have been the last boy chosen to play a game of softball, but I was always the first kid chosen for a team when it came time to paint the Thanksgiving or Christmas mural, and that made me proud. The only thing that did. I don't know if anything at Sunnyside ever made my big brother proud. If it did, he didn't brag or go on about it, and that would not have been like him.

AIRPLANES

IN THE SUMMER OF 1949 OR 1950 Tommy and I had our first airplane rides. Our uncle Bob knew a man, Frank Earhardt, who owned a 1946 Piper Cub Sea Scout. Knowing our fascination with flying (mine especially), Bob, ever the salesman, talked his friend into taking us boys up for a spin. We had to go one at a time since the Sea Scout had only two tandem seats, one for the pilot and one for a passenger.

Tommy went first, as usual. They taxied away from the dock, picked up speed, and lifted off the water. It climbed, banked to the left, and was soon out of sight. I waited for what seemed a very long time for that little yellow plane to return so it would be my turn to go up. I don't think ten minutes had passed when it touched down on Lake Chickamauga and taxied back into the Harrison Bay marina. When Bob and Daddy had it tied up to a cleat on the dock, Earhardt got out and helped Tommy out of the cockpit. He was smiling ear to ear and popped me playfully on the arm as he passed by me.

Then it was my turn.

We taxied out of the marina, took off to the west, and climbed up over the lake. It wasn't a long ride—we probably turned back four or five miles

Piper Cub Sea Scout, c. 1950

out, somewhere over Booker T. Washington State Park more than likely—but it was a glorious experience for me.

I SPENT COUNTLESS HOURS drawing airplanes, of which the Piper Sea Scout had become one of my favorites, along with my favorite warbirds—Corsairs, Spitfires, and Mustangs. I even equipped some of those with floats when it struck me to do so. I drew airplanes on everything I could lay hands on: stationery that Daddy or Uncle Bob brought home from their travels, wax paper from Mother's kitchen cabinet, butcher paper from the grocery store, paper sacks, walls.

Occasionally Daddy brought home long pieces of brown Kraft paper they used at his sporting goods store to wrap parcels. Tommy and I each took one or two pieces and drew alone, or if Daddy brought home only one long sheet, we often spread it out on the living room floor and drew together.

The drawings were usually based on the radio programs we listened to, like *The Roy Rogers Show*, *The Lone Ranger*, and *Sergeant Preston of the Yukon* (who flew a Cessna 310 named *Songbird* and was accompanied by his malamute, Yukon King, and his niece, Penny King).

But this was in the aftermath of World War II and so we based many of our drawings on the newsreels we saw at the movies: Paramount

News, Pathé News, the March of Time, and the many recurrent clips of victorious Allied battles in both theaters of the war.

Sometimes we based our drawings on the movies we saw: *Fighter Squadron*, *Battleground*, *Home of the Brave*, *Halls of Montezuma*, *The Desert Fox*, and John Wayne in the *Flying Leathernecks*. Of course, the sanitized film clips and the patently jingoistic movies gave us no sense of the true, horrific nature of war, so Tommy and I found it all very heroic and exciting, especially when the clips and movies involved aircraft and American victories.

We spread out the four- or five-foot piece of paper on the floor and lay down next to each other. Daddy sat in his favorite overstuffed chair, smoking his pipe and reading the evening paper, the *Chattanooga News-Free Press*.

Tommy, more often than not, was the Americans, and I was the Japs or the Krauts, unless I whined about it and he let me be the Americans. We drew our airplanes in flight. Bombers and fighters. Mine flying in this direction, his in that. We drew tanks and troops on the ground or ships and submarines at sea. We took turns opening our bomb-bay doors and dropping our bombs. We alternated turns opening fire from our fighter planes. All this was, of course, accompanied by the best sound effects we could muster. *Rata-tat-tat. KaBOOM! KaBOOM!*

Machine gun bullets were indicated by dotted lines that rarely went straight. We bent the trajectory at will in order to hit our targets. A drawing like this could take half an hour or better, and by the time Mother called us to the table for dinner, the entire surface was usually scribbled on and punctured all over where the crayons and pencils had torn through the paper in overly enthusiastic explosions.

Tommy always drew better than I did. That he was three years older than I was certainly a factor—though I think that his natural meticulousness had as much to do with it as anything.

When Tommy drew bombers he included details like insignias, machine guns and machine gun turrets, serial numbers, trim tabs, pitot tubes, antennae, and radio wires. And if his drawing was large enough, he drew in the flight crew. When his airplanes opened their bomb-bay doors, the bombs fell away in straight, evenly spaced, perfectly vertical files. Neat and orderly, his natural proclivity that would serve him well when, a few years later, he would attend a military school. I envied him and did my best to emulate his detailed and orderly drawings. I couldn't do it. My planes were drawn sloppily and disproportionately. My bombs fell away from my bombers in cluttered, backward-sweeping, ragged arcs rather than neatly spaced vertical rows like his. My bombs fell in graduated stages from the horizontal as they departed the belly of the plane to the vertical when they struck their targets—which, actually, is the way such bombs behaved. The best part of my drawings were the scrawls I made when my bombs struck their targets. But in trying to draw like he did, I think my skills improved, even at that age, like a tennis player who plays best against a better player. That meticulousness stayed with Tommy all his life. As an adult he spent hours polishing his shoes, cleaning his guns, and trimming his hair. Every Sunday he ironed fifteen shirts. Five for him and five each for his boys. His son Tyson told me that his Daddy put so much starch in their jeans before he ironed them that they could stand up all on their own. Nothing in Tommy's world was ever cluttered or messy—even the clothes in his closet were organized by kind and color, his shoes orderly on the floor—quite the opposite of his younger brother, then or now, whose closets are more like Fibber McGee's.

Our drawings were done when Mother called us to dinner,

"Tommy. Barry. Ches. Y'all come on in and sit down and eat now."

TOMMY'S DRAWINGS WERE informed by his methodical and military wont and sense of order, precision, control, and regularity—a perfectly valid point of view from which to work, and a sensibility that served him well in his life in the world of finance and real estate. Had Tommy gone on to become an artist I imagine him in the camp of Josef Albers or Frank Stella in the sixties, or perhaps one of the hyperrealists like Richard Estes or Richard Haden.

My drawings, on the other hand, were informed—or so it would seem—by logic, spontaneity, and observation, which is an equally valid point of view from which to work.

THERE WAS ONE DRAWING I remember doing all by myself lying there on Mother's Karastan rug. I don't know where Tommy was that afternoon, but I had this big piece of Kraft paper all to myself. Daddy was smoking his pipe and reading his evening paper as usual. Mother was fixing dinner in the kitchen. This was four or five years after August 5, 1945, and I was trying to draw a Boeing B-29 Superfortress as accurately as my ten-year-old skills allowed. I had seen a B-29 in a newsreel (probably the *Enola Gay* or the *Bockscar* since it was carrying an atomic bomb) and was struck by the rounded, heavily glazed nose assembly. I was drawing it as large as I could and imitating as well as I could my brother's use of insignias and other details. I drew the bomb-bay doors opening accompanied by a loud "skreeeeeak" that I thought might come from the metal-against-metal noise bomb-bay doors might make as they opened and locked into position.

Below the open bomb-bay doors, I drew one very large bomb. It was nearly half the size of the B-29 itself and was falling parallel to the fuselage, just like Tommy's bombs did.

On the side of this big bomb I wrote "A-TOMMY" in big letters because I thought it was named after my big brother.

THE MITCHELL

ONE SUNNY DAY IN 1949, Tommy and I were just home from school and were outside playing in the plum tree between our house and Floyd's. We had tired of our game and were lying in the grass trying to find animal shapes in the scattered clouds as they scudded overhead.

All of a sudden, a North American B-25 Mitchell, a World War II medium bomber, came into view from the north.

It was on fire.

We watched the white smoke trailing from the burning plane. It was losing altitude fast. We watched as men jumped, their parachutes opening and then dancing white against the cobalt sky. We saw something small fall from the plane, but couldn't tell what it was. Just before the plane disappeared over Missionary Ridge, the port engine fell off and we watched it drop, white smoke trailing after it. When the Mitchell passed from view, the smoke trails from the port wing and its lost engine dissipated in the early autumn sky. White parachutes bobbed and lingered below the scant, lazy clouds.

The plane was piloted by William E. Blair of Dallas, Texas, a thirty-year-old Army Air Force Captain. He had taken off from Augusta, Georgia, and was headed for Spokane, Washington. There were two other crew members, a copilot and a flight engineer. And there were six passengers aboard, all military policemen. An hour out of Augusta a fire broke out in an oil line inside the port wing. Blair dived to eight thousand feet trying to extinguish the flames, to no avail. At six thousand feet the fire had spread into the fuselage and Blair ordered everybody to bail out, which they did. Alone in the plane, Blair circled the city in an attempt to approach Chattanooga's Lovell Field, the municipal airfield that was only a few miles from where Tommy and I stood watching the drama unfold.

Magazine and newspaper accounts reported that the copilot parachuted safely and came to rest tangled up in a tree; that one of the MPs, Robert Hamby, slammed into the side of a bank building before landing on the sidewalk; that another landed on top of a school; and that yet another got caught up in telephone lines. Another man, Norman Henson, jumped from the rear of the plane, but his parachute didn't open. Nobody knows exactly what happened, but it seems likely that he failed to attach his parachute harness properly and when he bailed out it slipped off. He fell to his death in the playground of Ridgedale Elementary School on Dodds Avenue. Witnesses said that when he hit the ground he bounced six feet in the air and left a depression several inches deep in the playground. One horrified schoolboy who saw it happen reported that when Henson hit the ground there was a loud "pop" that sounded like a gun.

Henson must have been that small thing Tommy and I saw falling to the ground.

The disjunct engine fell on a house on East Twenty-first Street, tearing off a corner of the porch and part of the roof before hitting the ground six feet away. It was reported that it bounced ten feet into the air, and then rolled smoking into the street.

Blair's shirt, his captain's bars on the epaulets and identification cards in the pockets, was found on top of a car on Twenty-fourth Street. Both sleeves were burned. He must have ripped off his burning shirt and thrown it out the window. He stayed with the plane as long as he could, all the while desperately trying to find a field or some open space to set his dying aircraft down without killing a lot of people. He jumped at the last minute. The plane crashed into the east side of Missionary Ridge near the Bachman tubes on Highway 41. Captain Blair's body was found a few hundred yards from the smoldering wreckage of his Mitchell, the ripcord of his parachute was still in his hand.

When he got home from work, Daddy took Tommy and me to see what was left of the B-25. On the way Tommy and I were excited about seeing a real bomber up close. But when we got there, there was nothing to see but the clear-cut swath chamfered into the local vegetation, and parts of the plane strewn all over the hillside, some still smoldering. I can't say that either of us sensed the tragedy that all this implied, nor how much worse it could have been were it not for the remarkable courage of William Blair, but I can say that we were both very quiet as we surveyed the ravaged and blackened earth from which heat was still rising. Daddy tried to talk a cop into letting us get closer but we really didn't want to get any closer.

NIGGER TOMMY

RAIN WAS ABOUT THE only thing that could keep Tommy and me from playing outside in the summer, though some rainstorms invited us to build small and unsuccessful dams to hold back rivulets of rainwater that flowed down our short gravel driveway.

The backyard of our house was tiny compared to those of Velma's and Floyd's, but since the three yards were fenceless and contiguous it was like one big yard. A big yard attendant to three small houses, a dilapidated garage, a chicken coop, a badminton court, a rose trellis, a dog run, and an enclosed chicken yard where our aunt Grace raised chickens for Sunday dinners. Tommy told me many years later that watching her wring the necks of those hens on Sunday mornings was what turned him against eating anything with feathers on it.

It was in those yards that Tommy and I and the occasional friends, James Hoyt and Marlowe Mayfield, or Jimmy and Dickie Livingood, played dodge ball, passed footballs, and where I learned how to ride a bicycle. It was where, in summer, we captured June bugs, tied a piece of thread on a hind leg, and flew them in circles around our heads like tiny model airplanes. It was where on summer evenings Tommy and I caught lightning bugs, put them in mayonnaise jars with holes punched in the lids, and went to sleep with their eerie phosphorescence pulsating in the darkness of our room. We played cowboys and Indians and jumped out of Floyd's plum tree with bath towels tied around our necks pretending to be Superman or Captain Marvel. We rode our bikes up and down, and threw sticks and balls for Lady, Velma's German shepherd, and our runty bull-dog, Pinocchio. They were buddies, Lady and Pinocchio.

I wish my brother and I had been buddies, but we weren't. Now that I am old and Tommy is dead, I wish more than ever that we had been close when we were kids. But the fact is that my older brother played with me when he had nobody else to play with.

In the hottest part of the summer we ran a garden hose out to the side yard and filled a big galvanized washtub with water and splashed around in it. We hunched our thumbs over the end of the hose and squirted each other. We ran back and forth squealing through the spray and jumping in and out of the tub. If we got the grass too wet it turned sludgy. And if he happened to be home and noticed, Floyd came out and yelled at us.

"Go play somewhere else, goddammit! You're making a mess of my yard!"

One summer afternoon a little black kid stopped

and watched us. He stood on the gravel shoulder of Shallowford Road, peering over the top of the privet hedgerow that grew at the top of the yard, alongside the street. He must have been standing on tiptoe because all we could see was his head bobbing up and down, kind of peekabooing us.

And then he was gone.

I have often wondered what that little boy was thinking when he walked along our stretch of Shallowford Road. I don't know if he ever encountered Lady, who was rarely indoors or contained in any way, but if he did, he was apparently not afraid of her. Bob and Velma were proud of Lady, not only because she was a handsome dog, but also because she didn't like black people—or so they said. Or so they thought. And apparently the black folks who had to walk past their house thought so, too, because when they approached the Cox house they crossed to the other side of the street and stepped lively.

But if this little kid felt threatened by the dog he didn't show it. He could have stayed at home where it was safe, but he didn't. He could have taken the long way around our block, up and around on Haymore Street, but he didn't. He chose to walk on the same side of the street as our houses and to risk Lady's menace.

And then one day he was there again, peering over the privet hedgerow. He ventured—cautiously—into our front yard and stood next to the forsythia bush for a few moments, watching, weighing his move. Then he hollered at us,

"Hey! What y'all doin' down there?"

"Takin' a shower bath. What's it look like we doin'?"

"Can I come play wit y'all?"

Tommy and I looked at each other for a moment, not knowing what to say.

"I dunno," Tommy said. "Maybe. Lemme go ask Mother if it's OK."

I just stood there looking at this little kid, and he just stood there looking at me. We were both six or seven years old. Maybe a little older. We said nothing to each other, just looked. Kicked a little at the grass. Spat. It wasn't long before Tommy came out and told us that Mother said it would be OK, but that he couldn't come in the house.

So down to the side yard he came with us. Tommy and I had on bathing trunks but our new friend was fully dressed, so he took off his clothes, all except for his white underwear—a stunning contrast to his dark skin. He was not as sable skinned as Verneta, nor as light skinned as Arthur Boyd's tailor, Nap Turner. I had never before seen a black person so close to being naked and I wanted to touch him, to feel the texture of his skin that looked soft and satin, like he had been powdered with cocoa, but I did not.

We played until it was time for him to go home. As he was leaving Tommy hollered at him,

"Say, what's your name?"

"Tommy. What's yours."

"Tommy. He's Barry."

Our new friend Tommy came back a few times that summer, and the summer to come. It wasn't too long into that first summer when we had to make some distinction between the two Tommys. We all agreed that henceforth, little black Tommy would be called Nigger Tommy and that my brother would be just plain Tommy.

Nigger Tommy was a very pleasant kid, happy and good looking, too. Mother liked him and was glad that he came to play. He was always clean and dressed as well as we did, maybe even better. Mother explained to us that his clothes must be hand-me-downs from white people, or else his mama or grandmama must make them for him.

If Nigger Tommy was around at lunchtime, Mother made sandwiches and brought them out for the three of us to eat in the shade of the trees that bordered our little backyard. Mother would bring out a quilt or a chenille bedspread and smooth it out on the grass beneath her clothes-lines. Sometimes she would set up a card table and bring out folding chairs for us. She brought us ice-cold Cokes or iced tea or sometimes freshly made lemonade. She made fried bologna sandwiches, or tuna salad, but usually it was peanut butter and jelly because my brother was such a picky eater, though I have to say that we were all pleased

The other Tommy, c. 1947

when she brought out Vienna sausages and saltine crackers.

The three of us ate and laughed. Sometimes we laughed so hard that food and Coke spewed out our noses, and that just made us laugh all that much harder. We had fun, unaware that there were any differences between us other than the color of our skin and the fact that, as much as Mother liked the boy, he was the only one of our playmates who was never allowed in the house.

Then one day in that second summer he went away and we never saw him again. There were no good-byes. No last waves. No information about where he was headed or with whom. He just disappeared from our lives as suddenly as he came into them.

FAST-FORWARD TO DECEMBER 1962. Kay Richmond, a fellow student at the University of Chattanooga, and I were married. By the time we moved to New England in 1967, we had two small children, one of whom, Romy, was still in diapers and the older one, Cara, was barely out of hers. Our third daughter, Madeline, would come along a few years later.

I was teaching school in Massachusetts and over Christmas break we drove back to Chattanooga to visit family, though my family had broken apart after Mother died in January 1964. Tommy was living outside Nashville with his young family. Daddy had remarried and was living on Lookout Mountain. Christmas get-togethers were now a thing of the past for our Shallowford Road family.

In December 1969, Kay and I and the kids were home for Christmas and had a hankering for some honest-to-God barbeque, something that's all but impossible to find in New England, so we drove over to the Sportsman's Bar-B-Q Drive-In on Brainerd Road. I had been eating their sandwiches since I was a kid when their joint was out on Highway 58 just before you got to Lake Chickamauga.

It was a warm evening despite being late December. The sun was going down as we pulled our Kombi bus in and found a parking spot. Kay was holding Romy, and Cara was playing in the back. I beeped the horn to get the attention of a carhop.

A young black man about my age came over to the car to take our order. I recall that he looked a little like Cuba Gooding Jr.

I don't remember what Kay ordered, nor what we got the kids to eat, but I ordered what I almost always order: a pork sandwich with coleslaw and hot sauce, some beans on the side, and a tall glass of sweet tea with fresh lemon. As we waited for our food, we listened to Creedence Clearwater Revival, Neil Diamond, and Otis Redding playing on loud speakers. When the carhop brought our tray, it was balanced on one hand over his right shoulder and was overflowing with food and drinks—and a whole mess of napkins. I rolled the window up a few inches so he could anchor the tray over the glass.

I parceled out the food and we ate.

When we finished eating I beeped the horn and the carhop came to take away the tray. He hoisted it to his shoulder and turned to walk away. But then he stopped and turned back. He looked at me, adjusted the tray on his shoulder, and said, "You don't remember me, do you, Mister Barry?"

"No, I'm sorry. I don't." I answered.

"I'm Nigger Tommy."

This is, in fact, the end of the story as I recall it. I'm certain that I didn't just sit there like a knot on a log and say nothing, but I cannot imagine my responding with some kind of cordial inanity like,

"Oh, hey, Tommy, how you been? What you been up to, buddy?"

Given the way I feel about this story as I tell it today, I must have felt like I had just been punched in the gut. Tears well up every time I think about it, and I don't think that I'm all *that* different today from who I was then. The primary reason I expatriated myself from the South in 1967 was to escape the racism around me. My family. My church. The private school where I taught. I didn't have the personal, physical, or moral courage to go down to Alabama or Mississippi to help register voters, so I did the only thing I could. I left.

I never saw Tommy again. Nor did my brother. Many years later we were talking on the phone and this story came up in our conversation. Tommy told me that he thought, or had heard, that our friend Tommy had gone to medical school somewhere and was now practicing medicine. I would like to believe this, and perhaps it is true. But my brother was an errant—and arrant—storyteller who made things up when he wasn't privy to the facts or when the truth didn't suit him. I can't imagine why he would make up such a story, unless, as I came to find new layers to my brother's personality in our last years together, he was, like me, a recovering racist but never admitted it. Then again, perhaps he simply wished the very best for our childhood playmate of those summers long ago.

A SUMMER DAY

ON AN EARLY JUNE MORNING IN 1950, Aunt Grace's old leghorn rooster woke me up. He might have awakened Tommy earlier in the morning because he was sleeping with a pillow over his head. It was a cool summer morning—a happy morning, too, because we were on summer vacation, and any morning that I didn't have to go to school, vacation or not, was a happy morning. The air was clear as though there had been a hard rain during the night. The tall oak and black walnut trees growing alongside our house cast dark green, sun-dappled shadows over most of the dewy yard outside our windows where Tommy and I played. The chicken coop was on the far side of the yard in full morning sunshine. The white hens pecked and scratched at gravel, shit, and watermelon rinds, clucking all the while, and that cantankerous old rooster broadcast his authority to all in earshot.

Our bedroom windows were thrown open to the cool morning air. Soft, early breezes wafted the sharp, pungent odor of walnut husks rotting on the ground into our room. Through the window screen, with my chin in my hands and my elbows on the windowsill, I watched yellow and black caterpillars on the trees, some as big as your thumb, going up and down about their silent business while that nasty old leghorn went noisily and self-importantly about his.

My brother was thirteen that summer, old enough for Mother to trust him to take me downtown to see a movie and buy ten-cent hamburgers at the shiny white and stainless steel Krystal restaurant on the corner of Seventh and Cherry Streets. For thirty-five cents a person could get a cup of coffee and two tiny square hamburgers, a welcomed and affordable restorative at the beginning of the Great Depression. It is the oldest hamburger chain in the South. When I go back to Chattanooga I make it a point of eating a half dozen Krystal burgers in a single sitting, and I usually regret it.

After lunch Tommy and I went to a matinee at the Tivoli or the State movie theaters. I don't know what movie we saw this particular day but it was probably a Roy Rogers western or maybe an Abbott and Costello comedy. Mother gave us fare for the bus and money for hamburgers, the movie, and popcorn and candy.

When the movie was over we always walked up to Martin-Thompson Sporting Goods on Cherry Street, catty-corner from the Krystal. That was where Daddy worked, and if he was in town in the afternoon we usually caught a ride home with him. Sometimes it was a couple of hours before Daddy was ready to go. When that was the case Tommy whiled away the time trying out the new baseball mitts and gloves and admiring the hunting gear, especially the rifles and shotguns. I'd go around the corner and stare at all the model airplanes in the window of the hobby shop on Seventh Street, or I'd go back to the stock room and tear off large pieces of brown Kraft paper and draw. If Albert or Harvey, the two black deliverymen who worked for the store, were around I'd sometimes sit and talk. Daddy said Albert was a high yellow nigger who was too uppity for his own good. Daddy didn't approve of Albert's penchant for snappy clothes, his cocky attitude, or his shiny hair that was straightened and kept in meticulous place with a stiff pomade. But Albert was nice to me and told me stories about himself and his family. He aspired to become a podiatrist.

"Black folks always on they feet . . . you know what I mean, little man? Porters, conductors, maids, cooks. They always needin' somebody to take care of their feet."

But this particular Saturday Daddy must have been on the road selling or delivering football equipment down on Sand Mountain, Alabama (where the black delivery men did not go, afraid that they might not come back if they did), so Tommy and I caught the Eastdale bus and headed home.

It was hot and the bus was crowded. The seats

in the front of the bus were all taken, so we stood, my brother hanging onto the overhead handrail and I, too short to reach the handrail, was hanging on to him. Every time the bus stopped and started I was thrown off balance and jostled against the other people who were hanging on to the handrail like Tommy was. We'd not gone far when I saw an empty seat at the back of the bus. It was directly beneath the rear windows and a sign that read, THIS PART OF THE CAR FOR THE COLORED RACE. The empty spot was in the middle of the bench between two rather large black women. I pulled away from Tommy and made my way to the back and sat down.

One of the women was cooling herself with a cardboard fan that had a picture of Jesus on it . . . that 1941 Warner Sallman portrait of an Aryan Jesus that by then was making its saccharine way into every protestant church in America. Every now and again this woman's fanning tempo picked up as she tilted her fan a little toward me, inconspicuously. The extra little breeze was cool and welcomed. So was her smile.

Tommy was glaring at me as he clung on to the handrail with one hand. His free hand gestured what his lips were silently ordering me to do,

"Get your fat ass back up here with me, you little shit! Get it up here—NOW!"

When Tommy got really mad his eyes changed color, from the hazel color we shared, to a sour, yellow-brown like the color of the Beech-Nut tobacco juice Daddy spat. Tommy's anger made his bad eye worse, causing it to cross and to squint. I saw the fury in those eyes of his ordering me to get off my ass and come stand with him. But I did not. I stayed where I was because I was perfectly happy wedged comfortably between two big women, my feet dangling, not quite reaching the floor.

When the bus turned west off Tunnel Boulevard and onto Shallowford Road Tommy reached across and pulled the cord that rang the bell letting the driver know he wanted to get off at the next stop. In the few moments it took us to reach our stop, I considered not getting off at all. I was afraid of Tommy when he got mad, and I could just as easily get off at the next stop since it was only a short block farther up the road, right in front of Velma's house. I could have avoided my brother altogether had I done that. I could have gone in and visited with Velma for a while before going home. For all I knew Mother might have been visiting, as she often did, sitting out on the big screened-in front porch sipping iced tea and shelling peas or stringing beans.

When the bus stopped Tommy got off at the front. I got off at the back. The doors were sliding shut when he hit me. A right to my head. He hit me again as I was falling to the hot pavement. I sprawled into gravel and dusty grass, bleeding from my nose and mouth. Then he kicked me. I curled up in a ball and he kicked me again. And again. Through the ringing in my ears I heard him say,

"Don't you never sit with niggers again, you hear me, you little morphadite? You hear me? DO YOU HEAR ME?"

I lay whimpering, and did not answer him.

Then THUD! Another kick.

When he turned and walked away, I saw—through squinted eyes and tears—that his fists were still balled up. I sat up, tasting the iron of my blood mingling with the salt of my tears and the smells of hot summer tar and the diesel exhaust of the bus pulling away.

I heard Tommy whistle for our dog. Like nothing had happened.

KLAVALCADE

I NEVER HEARD THE *R* IN Verneta's name when I was a child. What I heard was *V'nita*—with a long *e* sound—and to this day when I say her name I pronounce it as I heard it when I was a little boy. The friendship between her and Mother never diminished over the years. In the privacy of our living room or sitting at the kitchen table they were equals and my mother treated her as such. Verneta called Mother "Billie" and Billie called Verneta "V'nita," just like everybody else did, even my brother and I. In the cooler months they sat and drank coffee; in the summer months they sat on the screened-in front porch and drank iced tea. I wish that I had listened to their conversations and could remember what they talked about, but I did not. I do remember that they got into arguments sometimes, but it never got heated and they never got angry with one another. I never heard Mother say, as she did to Tommy and me,

"Now you listen to me. . . ."

On the other hand, if there was a car in our driveway that Verneta didn't recognize, or if she knew that there was a stranger visiting—a preacher, say, or maybe a salesman trying to sell Mother a new vacuum cleaner, or a Christian

Science practitioner, Verneta would go to the back door and knock. She waited politely for "Miss Billie" to come let her in. She would not sit, nor was she invited to sit. In front of white company, Verneta would neither argue nor disagree with anything my mother said. It was always,

"Yes'm, Miss Billie" or "No'm, Miss Wilhelmina."

ONE SUMMER NIGHT IN 1957, Verneta did come to the front door while Mother and Daddy had company. They were playing canasta with family and friends and debating whether or not Jesus was really a Jew—the consensus among them was that he was not—according to Mother he was just a "dark, Mediterranean type."

Tommy, now a twenty-year-old with a red MG convertible and an endocrine system raging at full throttle, was out on a date with a woman named Maxine, who worked for our cousin Wayland and was ten years older than Tommy. We didn't see much of my Tom-catting brother in those days.

The living room windows and the door that opened to the front porch were propped open to let out the cigar and cigarette smoke, and to let in some fresh air. An old reciprocating fan grumbled on the floor and kept the smoky air circulating. The screen door of the porch was latched tight to keep out mosquitoes and moths. Lightning bugs blinked on and off in the front yard.

509 Shallowford Road, c. 1958

The quiet laziness of the card game conversation was suddenly interrupted by noise from the street. The Ku Klux Klan was parading up Shallowford Road in a "klavalcade," the term Klansmen use for a convoy of their cars and trucks, fond as they are of alliteration. It was a show of presence and power that typically preceded a cross burning somewhere. Everybody put down their cards and went out on the front porch to watch and wonder aloud where them good ol' boys there were goin' to go burn their cross that night. Somebody said,

"Be damned if I know, but I sure hope it's in some Jew's front yard."

I had come from my room at the back of the house to watch the show myself. We watched scores of beat-up cars and sorry-looking pickup trucks pass by, punctuated now and again by a shiny Cadillac or a new Lincoln. They were all in a slow procession up the street heading toward Missionary Ridge where several Jewish families and that well-to-do black dentist had fine homes overlooking the city.

The interior lights in the cars and trucks were on, or at least they were on in those that had interior lights that worked. Each car was full of Klansmen and Klanswomen in their hoods and sheets. There were children, too—Klanskids, I suppose they'd be called—dressed in miniature Klan regalia. One was riding on the hood of a car, leaning back against the wraparound windshield. Everything was moving so slowly the child wasn't likely to fall off, and even if he had he probably wouldn't have been seriously hurt. One of the lead trucks had a loudspeaker mounted on top of the cab. It amplified a man's gravelly, nasal voice that chanted, over and over—a harping drumbeat of rampant hatred, disguised fear, and ignorance.

"Nigga! Don't you never fergit yore place."

"Don't you never fergit yore place."

"Nigga, never fergit yore place."

"Never fergit yore place."

"Never fergit. . . ."

If there was more to the chant than that, I don't remember what it was. It eventually died out altogether. Diminuendo.

Everybody settled back into the card game. I was headed back to my room and stopped in the kitchen to browse in the refrigerator for something more to eat when I heard the front screen door slapping frantically against its latch. I heard someone crying, wailing, and trying desperately to get in.

It was Verneta. But before Mother could unlatch the screen door, Verneta pulled it apart from its hook and eye and burst into the brightly lit living room, blind with fear, and sobbing a litany of terror:

"Oh, sweet Jesus, Billie, what'm I gonna do?

What'm I gonna do? What'm I gonna do? What'm I gonna do?" Mother took her in her arms.

Verneta's sable skin was ashen, drawn, and streaked with tears.

Mother held Verneta tight and soothed her with gentle whispers and consoling pats and caresses on her back and shoulders.

"They're not after you, V'nita," Mother whispered. "They're not after you. You're all right. It's gonna be OK. Gonna be OK."

Floyd laughed condescendingly. Never looking up from his hand of cards, he said, "Billie's right, V'nita, they ain't after you. Them ol' boys there ain't got no problem with good niggers like you and your mammy. Now, that brother of yours, Leonard . . . he gets a mite uppity sometimes. You might wanna talk to that boy."

Everybody at the table grunted and nodded in agreement.

Then Floyd told Verneta to "go on back home, now. . . . You heard me. Go on."

She did as Floyd told her to do, and Mother went with her, across the street and up that long, steep hill in the dark.

Everybody else played canasta.

I WENT BACK TO MY ROOM and lay down on the bed and stared at the model airplanes that hung from the ceiling. Whatever I had been looking for in the refrigerator was still in the refrigerator. I couldn't eat anything. Verneta's face, distorted by terror and ashened by fear, was burned forever into my memory. I can see her face to this day, fifty-eight years later. Can see her mouth drawn down and terror struck, and I can't understand how she could have been as articulate as she was with her mouth so contorted. Can see her face nuzzled into Mother's neck as Mother tried to comfort her—and I imagine it looked much like it did when she was that little girl who stuck her head in the flour barrel so she could be white and go to a picture show with her little friend Billie, who was now holding her and comforting her again.

It may very well have been that night, it may have been that very event—the slapping of the screen door, the wails of terror, the gaunt pallor of despair—that began a series of awakenings inside me that initiated my ongoing recovery from racism. Had Tommy been home I don't know how he would have reacted. Would he, like Floyd, have laughed at Verneta and belittled her fear? Would he have shooed her out of the house so the card game could proceed without the unwanted distraction? Or would it have been an epiphany for him as it was for me?

PART TWO
ABOVE THE RIVER

How strange are the tricks of memory,
which, often hazy as a dream about the most
important events of a man's life, religiously
preserve the merest trifles.

SIR RICHARD BURTON
Sindh Revisited

BAYLOR

THE BAYLOR SCHOOL sits on a cliff high above the Tennessee River. Looking south you see Lookout Mountain in the misty distance as it looms high and humpbacked, seeming to brood on its historic past, the river beneath it, and parts of the city of Chattanooga, which lies at its foot on the other side of the river. In the Cherokee language, the name *Chattanooga* means "to draw fish out of water," but my brother and I grew up being taught that it meant "the eagle's nest."

Looking west you see the Grand Canyon of the Tennessee River, so called because the river cuts a deep gorge between the high wooded plateau of Prentice Cooper State Forest on the south and Signal Mountain on the north. In the distance it turns south and meanders out of sight behind Prentice Cooper and Raccoon Mountain. Storms coming up that gorge are breathtaking spectacles— as are the sunsets.

The Baylor campus is, without doubt, one of the most beautiful academic campuses I have ever seen anywhere. By comparison, the very prestigious Deerfield Academy, which is a few miles from where I live today, looks like a home for the impecunious.

John Roy Baylor founded the school in 1893. It

was originally called the University School of Chattanooga and was first located in the urban section of the city, but in 1915 the school moved to its present location overlooking the river. When the United States entered World War I in 1917 there was a need for educated young men for the military, and Baylor did its part by becoming an all-male military school. And so it remained until 1971.

TOMMY AND I were Baylor cadets in the 1950s. Just how we, coming from a not-so-well-to-do family who lived in a subaltern section of Chattanooga, were financially able to go to Baylor was a mystery for a long time. Daddy and Mother told us that we had been given football scholarships, which made no sense whatsoever, given that neither of us had ever played football. But Daddy's close friend Joe Engle, owner of the Joe Engle Bat Company in Chattanooga, was a talent scout for Georgia Tech's football team. He placed exceptional ball players from all over the South at Baylor for a postgrad year to prep them for Georgia Tech, so we figured that maybe he had pulled a few strings for us.

Neither Tommy nor I knew any better until a few years ago when a former classmate of mine, Sebert Brewer Jr., contacted me. Sebert was a trustee of the Benwood Foundation, a philanthropic organization founded by George Thomas

Hunter in 1944 as a perpetual homage to his uncle, Benjamin Thomas, one of the original owners of the Coca-Cola Bottling Company in Chattanooga (where the beverage was first put into bottles in 1899). When George Hunter died in 1950, 70 percent of Coca-Cola Bottling Company stock went to the foundation, just in time to benefit Tommy in 1951 and me in 1952.

Sebert called to tell me that the Benwood Foundation was initiating a fund-raising program and was contacting people who had benefited from it to give testimonials. He asked if I would participate. I did, and was happy to do so. This was the first I knew of the grant, and since it was an anonymous grant, I wonder if Mother and Daddy knew all along. If they did they never told us.

TOMMY WENT TO BAYLOR from 1951 to 1954, seventh to tenth grade. He dropped out after his sophomore year. Being two years older than his classmates was an issue that continued to eat at him, especially when a cadet officer who was younger, or perhaps the same age, dressed him down or called him "son" or "boy." Tommy *hated* that. His issues with reading still hounded him, though his skills in math were pretty good and would later serve him well as an officer of the Collateral Investment Company in Nashville.

I went to Baylor for six years, graduating in

1958. I'm sure that most people think that spending six years in an all-male military school would be tantamount to spending six years in prison, and in some ways I suppose that is true. Had I been an intellectually curious boy and a better athlete, my experience there might have been more rewarding. But despite the privilege and honor of going to Baylor, and despite the fact that it was eminently more stimulating than Sunnyside, I was neither intellectually curious nor athletically gifted. And neither was Tommy. Neither of us *caused* trouble, at least not intentionally, but both of us got into trouble from time to time. Nothing serious. We went where we were told to go. And we usually did what we were told to do—except for things like reading assignments and homework.

MOST OF MY MEMORIES from that time have the visual qualities of dreams: the images are slightly out of focus and dissolve at the edge. The palette is muted and nearly void of color. However, a few of those memories are clear and stand out in my mind's eye in full, lucid color, like photographs. They are sharp and crisp to the edge of the memory and beyond, vivid and salient dioramas, like my first day.

OUR FRONT YARD was in its usual morning shade from the large sweet gum tree that stood in the corner of our neighbors' front yard next to our driveway. Chickadees and sparrows flitted about here and there. It was about seven o'clock.

The grass in the shadow of the tree was wet with dew. I was apprehensive, and proud, as I stood on the front porch with Mother and Tommy. I was holding Pinocchio, who had just come back from one of his random scoots. Mother had dressed me as if I were going to the doctor's office—clean underwear and fresh socks with holes in neither, neatly pressed slacks, a freshly ironed shirt, hair parted and combed and held in place with Vitalis hair tonic. She was worried that Pinocchio was going to get my shirt dirty. I would get my first uniform in two or three weeks along with all the other new boys, except that mine was a used uniform and would be tailored to fit me well by Nap Turner. Tommy was wearing his uniform, as all old boys were required to do on the first day unless they had good reason not to.

The bus pulled up in front of our house, a small courtesy extended to new day boys on their first day of school. It was an International Harvester, I believe, painted battleship gray with the school's full name, THE BAYLOR SCHOOL FOR BOYS, lettered on the sides in red ten-inch-high Gothic letters. The folding doors squealed when the driver cranked them open. Mother stood watching, holding little Pinocchio in her arms. She might have been crying.

Tommy and I walked quickly across the wet grass, alert to fresh turds that the dog might have left behind. Tommy got on first. I got on after him, and seeing no familiar faces, I took the first available seat, which was behind the driver.

The hard leather seats were lumpy, cracked with age, and listed forward from years of use and misuse. Tommy didn't sit with me. He was as uncomfortable at Baylor as a whore in church and I think that this day I added to his discomfort. I embarrassed him, his little brother in his clean civvies and his Vitalis-stiff hair.

BAYLOR WAS ON THE other side of town, ten or eleven miles away from our home, and given all the starts and stops picking up students and the occasional staff member, it was about an hour's ride down McCallie Avenue toward town, across the river on the Walnut Street Bridge, on into North Chattanooga, through Stringer's Ridge tunnel, into Red Bank, and finally turning left off of State Route 8 to the lush and verdant Baylor campus. When the bus doors clanked opened, I stepped down onto the paved quadrangle of The Baylor School for Boys, and my life changed for all time to come.

NEITHER TOMMY NOR I was a stranger to the school. We had been campers at the Baylor Summer Camp, so we knew the campus as campers would, we knew a few older boys who worked as counselors, and we knew a few faculty members who oversaw the counselors and supervised various activities.

As a first-year day boy, knowing the campus and some of the older boys and members of the staff gave me a bit of stature and seniority over the other new cadets who were coming to the campus for the first time. What little seniority I had cut no slack elsewhere, because I, like all new boys —especially new seventh graders—was at the bottom of a very long and complex pecking order, a pecking order born out of normal adolescent, macho behavior, and the military mentality that permeated the school at that time.

All new boys were subject to harassments from upperclassmen. It was a tradition, a tradition that Tommy hated from his first day on campus. Depending on the degree of sadism in a particular old boy's psychological makeup, that harassment came in varying degrees of hectoring. My first experience of this tradition came on my first day. A small group of old boys noticed me and another new boy walking across the quadrangle before the first-period classes started at 8:00. And even though I knew the campus as a camper would know it, I did not know where the classrooms were, and we probably looked considerably confused and lost. They ordered us to stop and to stand at attention, never mind that we had not had our first lesson in military formation yet and were not in uniform. One of the boys bent down into my face close enough I could smell his breath. He growled at me,

"Boy, have you got your keys to the flagpole, yet?"

I was scared shitless. I had no idea what he was talking about.

"No."

"No, SIR, boy!"

"No, SIR." My voice quavered.

Another old boy put his face in mine.

"You been measured for your rifle yet, son?"

I was so scared I could hardly answer.

"No, SIR," I answered, looking at the ground. I had no idea what he was talking about either.

"Look at me when I'm talking to you, son."

"Yes, SIR."

I was about to cry.

It was not at all unusual for seniors to call underclassmen "son," or "boy," appropriating a slur usually reserved for black men—another reason it infuriated my brother so much when another cadet called him one or the other.

There were no keys to the flagpole.

All rifles are the same. No measurements are required.

But a frightened and nervous eleven-year-old kid knows no better. I suppose the japes went on until the school dropped the military program in 1971.

For the next four years my classmates and I endured harassments, large and small, lessening in degrees of torment each year until we became upperclassmen and graduated from harrasees to harassers. Tommy left Baylor before he had the opportunity to savor the experience from the other side of harassment. Once he left, he never went back. From that time on he had nothing positive to say about The Baylor School for Boys, and he spoke well of only a few teachers. He was disdainful of all his classmates except a very few. If Baylor had caught on fire, as the expression goes, Tommy wouldn't have pissed on it to put it out.

THE ACADEMIC DAY ENDED in the afternoon at 2:15, and unless it rained, we fell into military formation in the quadrangle or on the drill field at 2:30 and drilled for the next hour. On rainy days we spent the hour in class studying U.S. Army field manuals and committing the eleven General Orders to memory.

On the drill field we learned the School of the Soldier (moving, standing, turning, and marching as a single body—squads, platoons, companies, and battalions); we learned the Manual of Arms (standing, marching, and saluting with rifles); and those of us who eventually became cadet officers learned the Manual of the Saber (standing, marching, and saluting with the saber). My parents must have sacrificed to buy my saber.

There was no such thing as used sabers, as there were used uniforms. We all kept them. Today mine lives on the fireplace mantel in my library, CADET LT. ARTHUR B. MOSER engraved on its blade.

Having that saber—having *earned* that saber—was a consolation for Tommy's inheriting the sword our grandfather Albert LaFayette Moser was awarded for being the best drilled cadet at Sweetwater College, which was then a military school in Sweetwater, Tennessee. That sword is, and has been, an object of family myth for generations. In a letter dated July 15, 1932, my grandfather's brother, George, instructed his nephew, our father, to send him the sword. George told Arthur Boyd that the sword was Albert's soul and that Arthur Boyd was to prepare it for shipment according to George Moser's explicit instructions: "It is your daddy's soul," he said, "so do him this courtesy: Make a little case for it, make it look as much like a coffin as you can; Line it with gray, and cover the exterior parts with black, trim it with marigold and daises. Spend a little of his money of him who lived his life entirely in vain; express the achievement to me."

It never happened. Arthur Boyd ignored his uncle's instructions and the sword passed down to Tommy. Growing up knowing this, I was told that I would inherit our grandfather's knife, a little sword for the little brother. But there was never any such knife. My nephew, Todd Moser, is the current proprietor of Albert LaFayette Moser's sword and it rests today in his home outside Nashville and will eventually pass to his nephew, Andrew.

THE ONE THING THAT Tommy did seem to enjoy at Baylor, and to take pride in, was the uniform. We had to pay particular attention to our uniforms, and it was the sort of fastidious attention that suited Tommy well. He was good at it. He was downright enthusiastic about its presentation. He took a lot better care of his uniform than I did mine, and he looked better in it than I did.

Our gray wool trousers had black stripes down the outside seams. The blouse was the same gray wool. Black chevrons on the sleeve of the blouse indicated the military rank: the two lowest ranks (private first class and corporals) wore inverted-V chevrons on the lower part of the sleeve below the elbow. The higher ranks (sergeants, lieutenants, and captains) wore chevrons on the upper part of the sleeve above the elbow. Polished brass cross arms were worn on the lapels of our jackets and blouses. The blouse was cinched at the waist with a black leather Sam Browne belt. Our blue Oxford shirts were always pressed and heavily starched, the collar points held down with "Spiffies," wire apparatuses that fit under the tie and pinned into the collar points to hold them down and in place

Tommy Moser in Baylor uniform, 1954

invisibly. Our shoes were polished until we could see our reflection in them. I used spit with my wax polish, touching the polishing cloth to my tongue to help rub the polish into the leather. They looked fine, but Tommy's were always much better. He used spit and alcohol with the wax polish, and his shoes had the mirror perfection of patent leather. Some boys actually had patent leather shoes and Sam Browne belts that they wore for Wednesday inspections. Such accoutrements were well beyond Mother and Daddy's means.

Tommy and I spent hours on Tuesday nights polishing our gear to stand inspection the following afternoon, hoping that nobody stepped on our shoes between now and then. I remember Tommy sometimes wearing one pair of shoes and carrying his inspection shoes in a cloth bag.

During inspection the cadet officers and military faculty reviewed the entire cadet corps, critiquing haircuts, the polish of brass and leather, the creases in trousers, and the overall cut of our appearance. If we did not measure up, we were given detention. Some particularly well-groomed cadets were given a red Neat Cadet ribbon. As hard as I worked at it, I never—not in six years— won one of those little red ribbons. But Tommy won several before he dropped out. Tommy was good at looking good—then, and for the rest of his life.

• • •

AN HOUR AND A HALF of mandatory athletics came after drill. For me it was football in autumn, wrestling in winter, and track in spring. I was not good at any of it. For Tommy it was football in autumn and track in the other two seasons. He dreamed of being a great athlete. He had talent and speed, but no matter what sport he went out for there always seemed to be boys who were faster or had greater endurance than he did, and that did not do his self-confidence and self-esteem any good. He played football all four years he was at Baylor but never played above the junior varsity level, the team called the Baylor Midgets, the team I would captain my senior year, yet another source of filial animosity.

I was playing on the Junior Midgets when Tommy was playing for the Midgets the last year he was at Baylor. Occasionally the two teams scrimmaged with each other. In one scrimmage Tommy was playing center on a T-formation offense. I was playing middle linebacker on defense. As soon as he snapped the ball to the quarterback I shot the gap between him and one of the guards. I fully enjoyed showing him up and embarrassing him even if I did get fussed at by the coach because I wasn't doing what I was supposed to do. It infuriated Tommy because I was tackling the quarterback about one out of every two or three plays. He snarled at me,

"You do that again, goddammit, and I'm gonna cream your fat ass."

Well, of course I kept doing it. We were under the watchful eyes of several coaches and I thought that that would protect me from his wrath. It didn't. The next time I shot that gap he raised his elbow to meet my face. This was a few years before face masks were required, and his elbow found my mouth—and my two front teeth, and out they came—or *off,* I should say, right at the gumline. I've worn partial plates all but fourteen years of my life.

TO THE WORLD OUTSIDE Baylor and outside our family circle, Tommy presented himself in a brighter, if not completely honest, light. In one photograph I have of him he stands against a background of black walnut trees and a wire fence. He wears running shorts and a Baylor varsity track team jersey. In another, he's down on one knee wearing a Baylor varsity football jersey without shoulder pads and the standard issue, padded football pants. A football is on the ground in front of him. It's a classic pose that scores of Baylor players who went on to play in college or on professional teams copped, and whose photographs in that pose lined the halls of Baylor's gymnasium. In a third photograph, Tommy is on one knee again. He wears blue jeans, a jacket, and a western style hat, and is holding a

.30-.30 lever-action rifle in his right hand. In the left he holds a deer's head by an antler. The deer appears to be lying dead in dense foliage.

The thing is, I took all three of those photographs. I took them with Daddy's Kodak in various places around our backyard.

Unlike the misplaced and unfulfilled dreams manifest in the first two photographs I mention, the latter photograph was prescient: as an adult Tommy was a first-rate big game hunter. In his Hendersonville den he had the heads and hooves of every hoofed animal that lives on the North American continent, or so he told me. The trophies were truly abundant, so I don't doubt his claim. At the time of his death he was well on his way to bagging all the hoofed animals that live on the African continent as well.

At his funeral, the officiating minister—a big man with a deep, mellifluous Mississippi accent—said,

"You know, ol' Tom Moser wasn't much of a church-going man, but I really did like him. I played football, long time ago, at Ole Miss and Tom played at Georgia Tech, so we had that in common."

I remember nothing else from the preacher's homily because I was thunderstruck. Gobsmacked.

Later in the day, as people gathered at Tommy's place, I got to talking with my nephews, Todd and Tyson, and asked,

"You reckon that your daddy really did tell that preacher-man that he played football at Georgia Tech?"

A quizzical look came over Todd's face. Then he asked,

"Well, he did, didn't he?"

"No," I said, and immediately felt like a shithead. Why couldn't I just have kept my big mouth shut?

But instead of being angry, Todd chuckled.

"You know," he said, "that's just like Daddy. He'd tell a story and it'd be about this big" (his hands gesturing a smallish size), "and then he'd tell the same story again, and it would be this big" (his hands gesturing yet a larger size), "and then it'd be this big, and before long he'd get to believing it himself."

THE INTIMIDATION AND humiliation that Tommy endured for those four years at Baylor, whether real or imagined, or a combination of both, eventually drove him to quit. He had no desire to continue down that road, so he dropped out and went to work. He worked at menial jobs —washing cars, pumping gas, sweeping floors, stacking shelves—until he landed a well-paying job in Combustion Engineering's Chattanooga foundry. He made, and saved, good money. He bought a sporty little MG convertible. A red one.

A few years later, our cousin Wayland helped

Tommy find a job at American National Bank, where Wayland was, or had been, a teller. Tommy started as a runner, the lowest spot on the banking totem pole back then. But without the benefit of a college education—or even a completed high-school education—he worked his way up that totem pole. He became a teller, then a head teller, and eventually a branch manager. No one ever faulted my brother for lack of ambition, or determination, or for being stupid about money.

When Tommy died on July 19, 2005, he probably had twenty-five cents of the first dollar he ever earned stashed in a bank somewhere, or a coffee can. Our uncle Bob always said that Tommy pinched a quarter so hard that the eagle squawked.

The younger brother has never been frugal. Bob always said that money always burned a hole in my pocket.

THE BUS

THOSE OF US WHO LIVED far away from the campus spent a lot of time on the bus. An hour each way for Tommy and me and the other boys who lived near us. Longer than that for the boys who lived up on Lookout Mountain. Unlike the public buses, the more senior boys—officers, noncommissioned officers, juniors and seniors—reserved the back of the Baylor bus for themselves. When the bus entered Stringer's Ridge tunnel everybody ducked. It was a short tunnel, and the darkness, which came on suddenly, lasted only a few seconds. But the very brevity caused all hell to break loose—and furiously so. Only the boys in the back remained sitting up. Books and all manner of things not stowed or battened down flew through the air, hitting anybody who dared stay sitting up. Seniors turned the hefty part of their class rings to the inside of the palms of their hands and popped the younger kids on the backs of their heads. Hard. Cadet officers, under the pretense of maintaining or restoring order, meted out punishment by whacking kids upside their heads with their folded overseas caps. The caps themselves were limp, soft wool, and were harmless, but the officers' metal pips that were pinned to the front of the cap could, and did, inflict pain.

There were other, more sadistic, torments on the ride home that made the mayhem of Stringer's Ridge tunnel seem tame by comparison.

Sometimes a boy was forcibly stripped to the waist and held down while two or three other boys—all at the same time and in unison—slapped his naked stomach hard and fast until the boy's belly was red and raw. Other times a boy was stripped and pinned down while other boys rubbed the hair on his belly enthusiastically until it was all twisted up in small, tight pills of hair that had to be shaved off. Sometimes a boy was stripped of his trousers and forced off the bus in his skivvies to stand helplessly on the curb watching his trousers dangle out the bus window until they were dropped off a block or two from the unfortunate cadet's point of disembarkation.

Neither Tommy nor I was immune to these kinds of cruelties, but they befell us less often than they did some of the other boys, especially the ones considered odd or strange for one reason or another. I was more or less accepted into the clan because I accepted the established pecking order and I wasn't a wiseass—and perhaps because my fear of the bigger boys was mistaken for respect.

I was a short, chubby kid. Tommy was a tall, skinny kid. But apparently neither of us came across as being funny looking—a condition that was a certain invitation to abuse. I think that Tommy's being older probably played a part in

104

his being mostly excluded from the assaults, but for whatever reason, we Mosers suffered the humiliation of being put off that bus half-naked on Brainerd Road less than some.

When Tommy was in the tenth grade, his last year at Baylor, he was attacked on the way home. And who knows if this incident contributed to his making that decision or not? It was a Wednesday afternoon, and since neither of us were on varsity athletic teams we were free to catch the 4:00 bus that left campus right after inspection and go home. The early bus did not take us back to the point where it picked us up but made a straight shot east on McCallie Avenue, through the Missionary Ridge tunnels, and then went straight down Brainerd Road, stopping at designated stops to let boys off at whatever point was most convenient for them. We usually got off at either Seminole Drive or at Tunnel Boulevard and walked the mile and a half home.

This day Tommy, as always, was in his meticulously groomed and polished dress uniform. I remember that it was spring and we were in our white dress pants. Tommy was accosted just before we got to the tunnels. Those tunnels, unlike the tunnel through Stringer's Ridge, are long, and going east there is a slight grade. The old International Harvester was chugging along slowly and dutifully, and by the time we came out into the light at the other end Tommy had been stripped of his blouse, his pants, and his shirt and tie. At the next stop he was physically put off the bus. He stood there in his underwear watching his pants dangling out of a bus window. They dropped to the street along with his wool blouse and polished Sam Browne belt just as the bus shifted into first gear and continued on its way.

Given Tommy's penchant for grooming and his growing hatred for Baylor and the boys in it, he must have been hurt, indignant, and convulsed with rage. I did not get off the bus with him. I stayed on and got off at the next stop and walked home alone. I didn't want to be with him after that. I didn't want to give him the chance to take it out on me. I hated seeing him treated that way, but on the other hand I did take a little bit of enjoyment seeing him bullied.

EARLY IN MY SOPHOMORE year a funny-looking seventh grader playfully slapped me upside the head in the brief darkness of Stringer's Ridge tunnel. He was a short, fat kid who had an unruly head of black hair that grew down his forehead, terminating in the neighborhood of his eyebrows. He wore thick Coke-bottle glasses. Obviously he did not understand the hierarchical dynamics at play when he slapped me. I was in a bad mood because the juniors and seniors in the back of the bus wouldn't let me sit with them and it was the first year that Tommy wasn't on the bus with me, though I don't know what that might have to do with anything. Anyway, I hauled off and slapped him back. I slapped him *hard*. Really hard. Hard enough to break the bridge of his thick, black, horn-rimmed glasses.

As soon as he got off the bus he reported me, and rightfully so. First period had just begun when I was summoned to the commandant's office. I stood at rigid, chin-tucked attention while he upbraided me for responding to that innocent, playful act with such undueness. I was a cadet corporal when I went into the commandant's office, but I left it a cadet private—the same humiliating rank as the kid I slapped.

AS I GREW OLDER AND BIGGER, and as I increased in rank, both militarily and socially, I, too, became part of the hazing tradition, gleefully inflicting these traditional torments on the younger, more feckless, bus-riding day boys. Naturally, it was always done in fun—for the perpetrators anyway, as had always been the case.

As a cadet officer I was a seventeen-year-old fascist, having been well indoctrinated and initiated by five years of other young, dilettante fascists. I barked and hollered and screamed and prodded and poked and slapped my troops upside their heads just like I had been barked at and hollered at and poked and prodded and slapped upside my head when I was their age and of their

Barry Moser in Baylor uniform, 1957

rank and in their position. I can only wonder how my brother might have acted had he stayed the course and had become a senior cadet officer.

As the years went by the militaristic animus that Baylor instilled in me faded, just like the racism my family instilled in me. Less so with Tommy, though he did actual military service. I did not.

He joined the National Guard in 1960 and did his basic training at Fort Sill, Oklahoma. He did not join for patriotic or chauvinistic reasons. He joined to avoid being drafted, because he had no deferments. He was not in school nor was he married, so he was in a precarious situation vis-à-vis the Selective Service System. So he took the least risky route available to him and joined the National Guard and avoided being cannon fodder in Victnam, where he most certainly would have ended up had he been drafted.

I was fully invested in the military imperative when I left Baylor. Six years of military school coupled up with a family who wanted nothing more than for one of the sons to go to West Point (or, that failing, to become a doctor, lawyer, or minister) and you have a solid martial foundation that I was eager to build on. I wanted to be a fighter pilot more than anything I could think of, and would have joined the U.S. Air Force had I good eyesight. But I had poor eyesight. And if I couldn't be a fighter pilot, I didn't want to be anything.

In June 1966, one of my best friends from Baylor, Parks McCall, a radar systems operator in the backseat of an F-4C Phantom jet, was killed in Vietnam. And with his death all the spit and polish that the Baylor School for Boys and my family had put on the face of things military became tarnished.

And my life's direction shifted dramatically.

I found myself siding with the antiwar movement, though I did so mutely, wary of familial and societal repercussions. And at the same time I found myself sympathizing with folks who were sitting in at Woolworth's. Again, mutely. My obvious cowardice would not have served me well in military service.

I MANAGED TO STAY a step ahead of the draft, though not by virtue of any kind of plan. I had been a preacher in college as well as a student, so I was deferred. After college I was no longer a preacher but I was married and had started teaching and both of those conditions were deferments. Then the babies came along. Eventually I was too old for the draft.

I was a student at the University of Chattanooga when I first began examining my family's teachings about race. I was the second person in my family to go to college (Albert Moser being the first), and that opened up worlds hitherto unknown to and unseen by me. It was while I was at university that I received my license to preach in the Methodist Church. I embraced Christianity with a fundamentalist's zeal, and as I read and reread and reread the Gospels, paying particular attention to the teachings of Jesus, especially the Beatitudes, I began to seriously question the values of my family, the values of the society in which I lived, and the values of my church community. And as I reexamined those values, I was being exposed to new values and ideas, primarily under the guidance of Bill Brockman, the director of the Methodist Student Center at the University of Chattanooga. Under his influence, and that of the students who gravitated to him, the scales of prejudice and bigotry began to fall from my eyes, much as the scales of blindness fell from St. Paul's eyes on the road to Damascus.

Tommy, on the other hand, stayed faithful in the racist tack that both of us had been harnessed with. Or, perhaps, so he would have had me think. Toward the end of his life I began wondering if the abusive racial slurs he threw at me in every conversation were really as malevolent as he wanted me to think they were. When he spoke well of the Ku Klux Klan, was he really of that mind, or was he putting me on knowing how much I despise them?

SKIRMISHES

MOTHER TOLD A STORY about Tommy's breaking a carton of eggs over my head when I was an infant. She said that I was in the front seat of Arthur Boyd's car, propped up on pillows, when Tommy took the carton out of the grocery bag in the backseat and broke the eggs, one at a time, on my little bald head. The car was parked in front of the Haggard grocery store, where I assume Mother bought the eggs. Arthur Boyd had gone in to buy some smokes. Mother was standing on the porch visiting with a neighbor and wasn't paying close attention to what was going on not ten feet from her. Tommy had managed to break several of the eggs before Mother noticed and put a stop to it. For all I know I might have enjoyed it.

I can't say for certain, but that could have been the beginning of our life of general conflict, because when I was a kid I thought that Tommy sometimes beat me up just for exercise and for the fun of it. And for the longest time, I wouldn't fight back. Mother told me to stand up to him. She said that if I did, he'd leave me alone. She told me that many times as she wiped away my tears. But I would not stand up to him and he did not leave me alone. The immutable facts of the three-year difference in our ages and his being only a year ahead of me in school undoubtedly played a part in his acrimony toward me, and until I was sixteen or seventeen I simply took whatever he dished out, even if I had to ball myself up to protect my face, hoping that Mother—or someone—would come to my rescue, or that Tommy would just stop it, go away, and leave me alone, which he sometimes did. My usual retaliation was to tell on him, hoping that Daddy or Mother would mete out whatever punishment they thought he deserved—which was usually having his allowance suspended (we both got fifty cents a week) or being confined to his room, which, being *our* room, meant that I was locked out of it. What I really hoped for was that Mother would make him go cut a switch from the forsythia bush. We were never really whipped, or spanked (other than with Daddy's harmless hairbrush), but occasionally Mother did make us cut our own switches, and forsythia branches are very long and very limber.

As we got older our fights usually began with bouts of name-calling, then graduated to pushing and shoving contests, then punches were thrown to the shoulder, gut, or groin. As a kid, I never threw that first punch. Every time I thought about hitting him in the face, the muscles in my arms grew leaden. The best I could muster was a shot at his shoulder. Usually our fights ended up on the floor in a wrestling match.

For fourteen years Tommy and I shared a

bedroom. Mother favored pastel colors, so our little room was a pastel green. There were twin double-hung windows that faced west. The windows were dressed with white curtains and white, wood-slatted venetian blinds. Tommy's bed was tucked into the corner of the room away from the windows. My bed was right next to them. The beds, maple four posters, were made up with matching chenille bedspreads, when mine was made. Tommy was a lot better about making up his bed than I was. He was better organized, too, from the clothes hanging in the closet to the socks organized in his sock drawer. His things were rarely out of place. For me, things were kicked under the bed and jammed into whatever drawer had room. Out of sight, out of mind. There were two chests of drawers, one for each of us, and a cotton rug on the wood floor between the beds. At the foot of his bed was a nightlight that was left on every night. Ever since our great-aunt had punished Tommy by locking him in a closet, he had been afraid of the dark.

Above my bed hung a dozen model airplanes, maybe more. They hung from the ceiling by a tack and a length of string. If Tommy hung any models above his bed I don't remember, but if he did there were not many. Maybe one or two. Making models was not his favorite activity as it was mine. There is a photograph I have of him as a boy of eight or nine standing at the end of his

Model airplanes

bed in dark slacks and a white long-sleeve shirt and what looks to be a tie. He's holding a broom and smiling broadly.

Picking up our room was an occasion for mayhem. I was good at making messes, but not so good about picking up after myself. Tommy could tolerate my slovenliness just so long. When we were very young he would tell Mother that I had shoved a mess of some sort under the bed and she would come and make me clean it up. As we got older Tommy took it on himself to make me keep my side of the room tidy, and to his standards of tidiness. Our rows over neatness intensified to the point of becoming unbearable for Mother.

In the midfifties Mother and Daddy enclosed the back porch intending it to be a family room, and for a year or two that's what it was used for. But when our fights got to be too much for Mother to handle, they let me have the back room for my bedroom, and only Mother fussed at me about keeping it neat.

Mother never fussed at Tommy about keeping his room neat. She didn't have to. Tommy always liked things neat and orderly: his person, his environment, the bombs he dropped from the belly of his imaginary bombers. If there had been such a thing as a "neat cadet" ribbon in the real world, my brother would have had a chest full of them. Spit and polish got into his bloodstream early on.

I, on the other hand, was, and still am, more like Nap Turner, whose tailor shop was calculated pandemonium. My sense of order is to stack things in piles. To keep up with Tommy, I would have had to cut too deeply into the time I had to draw and build models. Not much has changed. There are stacks of books on tables and on the floor of my studio. To look at my drawing table, my desk, the counters you would think that I could never find anything, and sometimes that is precisely the case. But most of the time I know where things are. When I don't I wish I were more like Tommy.

SOMETIMES OUR FIGHTS began when Tommy ordered me to do something that I did not want to do. I was stubborn, if not pugilistic.

One summer morning, 1956 or 1957, I was in Bob's basement workshop about to apply varnish to a coffee table that I was making for my room. Bob was at the lake fishing with Daddy. Velma was upstairs alone, watching television or puttering around in her kitchen. Without any warning Tommy stormed through the door and said,

"I need you to come with me down to the house, now."

"Why?"

"I need you to help me clean out the gutters."

Had I dropped what I was doing and gone with

him everything would have been copacetic. I hated taking orders from my brother, especially when I was doing something I wanted to do that didn't involve him. I said,

"I'll be along in a minute, just as soon as I finish doing what I'm doing."

He growled something at me and left. I locked the shop door from the inside and went back to my work. He came back in half an hour or so, and when he found the door locked, he started pounding on it and thundered at me,

"Get your fat ass in high gear and come help me."

I didn't respond.

"Open this fucking door."

"Go fuck yourself."

Oh, God, did that send him into a deep, almost maniacal rage. He kicked and pounded on the door until the lock gave way. I dropped the paintbrush and turned to face him, determined not to let him do anything to ruin my table, something that he was certainly capable of. More than once, in fits of rage, Tommy smashed a model I was building or tore up a drawing.

Two steps led down to the shop floor and before he got to the second step I tackled him, hauled him up on my shoulders and drove him out into the yard. His back caught an exposed lightbulb that broke and cut him badly enough to bleed but not seriously enough to warrant first aid. He was pummeling my back with his fists and trying to get in a position so that he could hit my head or face. He was screaming and yelling at me,

"Fight me fair, goddamn you, you chickenshit, fight me fair!"

Tommy was six-foot-one with long arms. I was five-foot-eight with short arms. He had a good five- or six-inch reach on me, so there could be no such thing as a fair fight standing toe to toe with him. The only thing that equipped me for a fair fight was my training as a wrestler at Baylor, and even though I never won a match, I could still hold my own.

I threw him on the dewy ground in the shadow of the house, but I didn't turn him loose. I tied him up in some now-long-forgotten wrestling hold and it felt good being the one doing the pinning for a change. His eyes were a yellow tempest of fury, but since he had never wrestled, he didn't know how to get away from me.

"Let me go, you fuckin' chickenshit!"

I had him tied up so tight he could hardly move. My face was inches from his and I had my right hand free. I said,

"You know, I could beat the shit out of you right now if I wanted to."

"Go ahead. You're too goddamned chicken."

He was right.

Lady barked and nipped at both of us as we

struggled in the wet grass. Velma heard the ruckus and came down her back steps wringing her hands and pleading with us to stop.

"I'll have a heart attack if y'all don't stop that right now. You wanna see me dead? Oh, oh, oh, God! Stop it! Stop it!"

Had I been she, I would have turned the hose on us, as I would on a pair of fighting dogs, but she just stood over us wringing her hands and wailing.

"I'm willing to quit if you are," I said to Tommy.

"OK. OK. Just turn me loose."

I turned him loose and stood up. When he got to his feet, he took a big swing and *wham,* his fist found my face hard and I went down. He stormed away. I went back to my work with a bloody and swollen lower lip. I never did help him with whatever it was that he wanted help with.

I wish that there had been some kind of "equal and opposite reaction" to the violent episodes that blew up between us. Somehow. Sometime. But there were not. Certainly there were days, even weeks of détente, but there were never any explosions of brotherly affection. If there were brotherly embraces I don't remember them. There were no shared confidences. No solidarity that might have balanced and ameliorated the violent episodes. That might have softened the edges of the rift that would continue to ossify over the next five decades.

ANOTHER SUMMER SATURDAY, an afternoon this time, Mother was away visiting a friend and doing her grocery shopping. I was in my back room drawing and listening to *Saturday Afternoon at the Opera*. Tommy came in and demanded that I help him bathe Penny, our collie. It was his idea to bathe her, not Mother's, and certainly not mine, but he insisted that I help him.

I refused.

He hit me.

I tackled him, and the fight was on.

The altercation migrated from my bedroom into the back hallway, through the kitchen, across the dining room, and was in full tilt in the living room when Mother came home.

When she came in and saw her dining room chairs overturned, the living room floor lamp in pieces on the floor, the door leading to the hallway broken, and a hole in the living room wall. She screamed and pleaded for us to stop. We would not.

She phoned Floyd, who happened to be home that afternoon, and begged for help. By that point our fight had been going on for a half an hour or better.

Floyd was a tall, strong man, a chain-gang boss who was used to dealing with convicts. But when he tried to separate us, we turned on him in a rare moment of brotherly solidarity. I don't know why, but perhaps our shared, pent-up anger at him for his years of sullenness and irascibility toward us kicked in. No matter, we took him by his arms, dragged him out onto the front porch, and threw him bodily into the front yard. I wonder why Tommy and I did not establish an immediate détente and start laughing our asses off at this little victory over our tyrant uncle, but we didn't. We just went back to shoving and pushing and calling each other the foulest names we could think of. Floyd must have been humiliated because he went home quietly and without offering any further assistance. Mother never asked him to break up another of our fights.

Now she was frantic. She was at the end of her rope (as she was wont to say), and as a last resort, she called the police. Ten minutes later, the fight was still under way, but by that time we were exhausted and it was more pushing and shoving and more name-calling. We both wanted to quit, but couldn't.

The police officer arrived and parked his black cruiser in the front yard. He left the red bubble-gum-machine beacon on the roof flashing. When he came in, Mother took him by the arm begging him for help. The presence of a policeman in our living room was enough to make us stop our brawl. He did not threaten us in any way, other than keeping his hand on his nightstick, but he did warn us that he could, and would, haul our sorry asses in and book us on any number of charges if we ever did this again. The idea of spending time in a Chattanooga jailhouse was plenty sobering. The officer left. I went to my room. Tommy to his. Never mind the broken furniture.

YOU WOULD THINK THAT age and maturity would have diluted the animosity between us, but it did not. At least not altogether. Our fights became less frequent, given that I had been away in Alabama studying at Auburn and Tommy had been away in Oklahoma for Basic Training at Fort Sill. Our paths simply did not cross very often.

But then that, too, changed.

In 1961, Daddy was hired to be the manager of the Chattanooga Golf and Country Club and one of his perquisites was a handsome two-bedroom apartment on the second floor. A large picture window in the living room overlooked the Tennessee River and Missionary Ridge beyond. But it meant that, once again, Tommy and I would share a bedroom.

I was in my final year at the University of Chattanooga and was working as assistant minister at Newnan Springs Methodist Church in north Georgia. I was recently engaged to Kay, who had moved to Chattanooga from Cape Girardeau, Missouri, two or three years earlier.

It was a Sunday afternoon and Tommy had been to his weekend drill with his unit of the Army

National Guard. I had done my morning duties at Newnan Springs and was killing some time before going back for my Methodist Youth Fellowship meeting and the evening services.

I was lying on my bed reading a *Mad* comic book. He came in and was in a foul mood. He had been up since before dawn. He was tired and wanted to rest, so he slapped the comic book out of my hands and stood over me.

"Get the hell out of here, I want to take a nap, asshole. Go somewhere else to read your god-damned comic book." What I really wanted to tell him was, *Shove it up your ass, I'm not going anywhere.* But being a newly minted preacher boy, I had cleaned up my penchant for profanity and said,

"No."

By this time Tommy was reluctant to hit me, knowing that I was no longer going to take his abuse without some sort of physical reaction in like kind. I don't think that he entirely trusted my new "turn the other cheek" philosophy, so he started bad-mouthing Kay.

And I was getting *really* irritated. Hc was in a rant, and then he said,

"You know, you used to be a pretty good kid until you took up with that Yankee bitch, Kay."

By this time I was sitting on the side of my bed. He was standing, looking down at me. His fists were balled up. The name "Kay" had scarcely passed his lips when I brought my fist to meet his mouth and nose. I hit him so hard he flew backward across his bed, bounced against the wall beyond that, and crumpled to the floor. By this time Mother came in and pleaded with us not to fight. She didn't want any club members to hear, afraid that it might impact Daddy's new position. I went to the back porch to finish my reading. Tommy got his way, but not without payment.

That was the first and only time that I ever hit Tommy before he hit me, the first time I ever penetrated what Andre Dubus III refers to as breaking "through that invisible membrane around another's face." And it proved that Mother was right all along: I stood up to him, I cold-cocked him, and that put an end to physical altercations between us for the rest of our lives. I wonder what our relationship might have been if I had coldcocked him at an early age, if I had cracked a bunch of eggs on his head, if I had had the courage to just let go and swing at his face. Bust his lip or his nose and let him taste the salty iron of *his* blood.

Looking back through the long lens of time, I can't imagine that the issues that fueled our skirmishes were very different from those of a lot of siblings. Perhaps most, even. I remember my two oldest daughters fighting a lot in their teen years, but their bones of contention usually begot nothing more serious than a few weeks—or months—of their not speaking to each other. I remember thinking how silly it was for them to fall out over unimportant things. The long lens of time becomes blurred when I look back hoping to fathom why what seems to have been ordinary postadolescent discord between Tommy and me prompted such violent and physical conflicts that were so completely out of proportion with the cause of them.

BRIDGES

DESPITE THE DIFFICULT TIMES, Tommy and I had moments that bordered on the fraternal. I went hunting with him. And fishing, although if it were possible to decline an invitation to go fishing, I declined. I hated fishing. Bored me to death. I much preferred staying home to draw or to build a model. I hated fishing so much I'd go to church to avoid it.

But when we were very young Velma liked to take us carp fishing down on Chickamauga Creek. The creek was only a couple of miles from our house, and sometimes we'd walk, carrying our poles, bait, and lunch. We often stopped and picked blackberries along the side of the road. More often than not, we drove to our fishing hole in her black Model A roadster. Tommy and I shared the rumble seat, a treat we never tired of. Nor did we ever tire of the "ahooga" sound of the horn.

Our hole was in the shade of a rusting old Pratt truss bridge. The bank was packed red dirt and was downright slick in some places. The bank on the other side was overgrown with wild hydrangea, swamp milkweed, and elderberry. The whole of the creek, which was always a café au lait color, was vaulted by an understory of tall river birch, sycamores, elms, and willow trees. The tiny waves made quiet, gentle sounds as they slapped rhythmically against the bank. Iridescent snake doctors darted and hovered above the water and then darted off again, often paired and flying as one. We did not swim in that water, ever, because it was a well-known fact (or myth) that Chickamauga Creek was home to resident cottonmouths. Southeast Tennessee is not the normal range of the western cottonmouth, but people often talked of seeing them, and it's not a big stretch to imagine a few fugitives making their way up from north Georgia. Of all the times we fished that shady hole, we saw only one, we thought, and that was from the safety of the bridge.

The fishing poles we used were right out of *Adventures of Huckleberry Finn*. Old cane poles. No reels or anything, just a line with a hook and sinker tied to the end. If we were feeling lazy, we put a red-and-white bob on our lines, stuck the poles in the ground or wedged them between rocks, and lay back and dozed in the cool mottled shade. When Velma packed our lunch she packed a whole loaf of fresh sandwich bread. After eating sandwiches, peanut butter and jelly usually, she rolled up the leftover bread into tight, dense dough balls for bait. Carp adore them, and we caught a few every time, but we threw them all back. I asked Velma one day why we ate catfish but not carp, and she said,

"Honey, only niggers eat carp."

However, I did find that running trot lines and juglines with Daddy was fun. We were not just sitting doing nothing but drowning worms. We were doing something most of the time—pulling up the lines, harvesting fish, and baiting large hooks with big chunks of raw beef. And we almost always caught a few catfish, and I got to clean them when we got home. This was one job that Tommy refused to do. Catfish don't have scales like crappies or bass. They have skin very much like a shark's skin and the skin has to come off before they are cooked. It was my job to clean and skin them. For a boy intensely interested in biology this was not a terrible chore. I cut the belly open and scooped out the entrails with my hands and slopped them into a bucket that then went to Grace's cat and chickens. I put the fish on a wooden plank and drove a nail through its head and into the plank to secure it. I made a V-cut with my knife right behind the skull and then scraped up a bit of the hide and pulled the skin off with pliers. It doesn't come off easily. That's why you nail the head to a plank. Tommy couldn't stand being in the basement with me when I cleaned catfish. Made him sick. May have been a reason why he wouldn't eat anything that had fins, either.

ONE SATURDAY MORNING not long after Tommy got his driver's license he asked me to go crow hunting with him. We drove out north on Tunnel Boulevard and turned off onto a dirt road that led up to the foot of a low ridge that over-looked Chickamauga Creek in places.

Crows are notoriously difficult birds to shoot, and even more so if you don't know what you're doing, and we did not know what we were doing. Tommy had a shotgun, Daddy's 12-gauge Remington 870, and I had a Remington, too, but mine was a much smaller .410/.22 over and under: a double-barrel gun that has a .410 shotgun barrel on bottom and a .22 rifle barrel on top. There's a little barrel selector button on the right side of the gun. If the selector is in the up position the hammer fires the "over" barrel, the .22. If it's in the down position the hammer fires the "under" barrel, the .410 shotgun barrel.

It was early fall and the leaves on trees were just beginning to turn color and the sunlight was dappled on tree trunks and forest floor. We took a path that stayed mostly on the crest of the ridge, Tommy's gun at the ready, mine on my shoulder. We walked for a good while and heard a lot of cawing, but we didn't see any birds. A few minutes later, still walking the path, we spotted one. It was perched on a tree branch close to the trunk. Tommy shouldered his 12-gauge. Just as he squeezed the trigger the crow stepped behind the tree trunk. Didn't fly away, just ducked behind the trunk. The pattern of the gun's shot tore away a good part of the tree where the crow had been. My ears were ringing and the air was thick with the smell of cordite. Then that damned crow stepped out in the open on another branch, turned away from us, twitched its tail like he wanted us to kiss it, bobbed, and flew away.

The morning grew long and then it was time for us to get back home. We heard lots of crows, saw lots on the wing, but saw only that one bird in the tree. I had not fired a shot the whole morning, so when a blue jay landed on a limb above me I shouldered my little Remington and squeezed off a shot. I thought the barrel selector was in the up position, but it was not. To my surprise the shotgun barrel fired and once again the air smelled of cordite, my ears were ringing, and the air around us was a blizzard of blue and white feathers.

That was our one kill for the day. We were laughing about it when we got back to the car and headed home. We never again killed anything when we hunted together.

A FEW YEARS LATER we went crow hunting again. Tommy was twenty-one, I was eighteen. I was home for the Christmas break from Auburn, where I had begun college in September. It was New Year's Eve and I was going to a big party up on Lookout Mountain that night with some old Baylor buddies. It was midafternoon and Tommy and I were bored watching a football game that wasn't very interesting. The sun and blue sky outside were a lot more inviting than a boring football game on a black-and-white television set, so we decided to go shoot crows.

I was the odd one in the family in that I was never much interested in guns any more than I was fishing gear. But guns were a significant part of my Baylor education, and at home they were plentiful and hard to ignore. Daddy and Tommy had a collection that ranged from a bolt-action 30-06 to the German 9mm Mauser rifle that Daddy's brother gave him. We had handguns, too, a German P38 Luger and a .38 Colt snub-nosed revolver that was kept loaded in a holster on a belt that hung from the bedpost on Daddy's side of the bed. At Baylor I became intimately familiar with the anatomy of my M1 Garand and as a senior was checked out with it on a Chattahooche, Georgia, firing range. I did moderately well but was a far cry from being a sharpshooter. The only guns that ever belonged to me personally were my Daisy BB gun, my Red Ryder air gun that I had as a little boy, and a .22 revolver that I bought before leaving Tennessee in 1967, took to New England with me, and eventually gave away.

Tommy chose Daddy's pump-action 20-gauge shotgun, and I packed the same little Remington .410/.22 over and under that I always took. It was an unusually warm day for that time of the year,

Crows in a field, December 31, 1958

so I slipped on a thin jacket over the white T-shirt I'd been sitting around in. We packed the guns into the trunk of Tommy's MG convertible and headed out toward the airport with the top down.

When we got out near what is now the Vulcan Materials stone quarry, we parked the car, put the top up, and took out our guns and a box of shells.

We had learned a bit more about crow hunting since our hunt a few years earlier, so we waded out into a field of high grass where, near the middle, there was an uprooted tree. We decided to use the tangled old tree as a makeshift blind, so we crawled in among its twisted and broken limbs and settled down. Once we were situated and still, Tommy began blowing on the wooden crow call Daddy had given him for Christmas. I was standing behind him, holding my gun in my left hand. My right hand was in the pocket of my jacket. For no particular reason I shifted my weight from my right foot to my left and put the gun in my right hand. At that precise moment I felt a snag at my jacket. A fraction of a second later I heard the report of a rifle.

Up near the edge of the field near where we left the car, there was a person with a .22 rifle. When he heard Tommy's crow calling he squeezed off a shot in the direction of the cawing, hoping, I suppose, to scare up whatever crow or crows that might be hanging out in that derelict tree.

That random bullet went between my right arm

and my rib cage and ripped through the pocket of my jacket where my hand had just been.

We scrambled out of that dead hackberry tree as fast as we could and chased down the guy who had fired the shot. He was a kid about our age and I was afraid for him. Tommy rarely got into fights with anybody but me, but this afternoon I thought my big brother might hurt this boy. I was thinking about hurting him myself. In fact, I wanted to stomp the living shit out of him right there and then.

"What the hell were you thinking, asshole?" I said.

But the poor guy was so scared and upset when he found out what had happened he started shaking. So we tried to comfort him.

"No harm done, buddy," Tommy said. "Close call, that's all."

We asked his name. He said, "Turner."

I don't remember his first name but it turned out that he was the son of our fourth-grade teacher. She was a wonderful person, my absolute favorite of all six of my Sunnyside teachers. Tommy's, too.

When I got home I took off my jacket and was about to clean my gun even though it had not been fired, when Tommy said,

"What's that?"

"What's what?"

"Those holes in your T-shirt," he said.

"What holes?"

I looked down and saw two small holes about an inch apart. Turner's bullet not only went through my jacket's pocket, it went through my T-shirt as well—but it did not touch my skin.

So many things about that day were seren-dipitous, and they called for introspection. I did not go to the party that night. I stayed close to home.

So did Tommy.

PART THREE
BROTHERS

Love is not love that can only love those already flawless. That kind of love requires no enlargement of the self: It requires no love.

ANDREW HUDGINS
The Joker

Tommy with Uno, our cousin's pup, c. 1951

ONE

ON THE SECOND DAY OF December 1997, my brother phoned me from Nashville. I was working on an illustration for a new, upcoming Pennyroyal Caxton Press edition of the King James Bible, and was deep into engraving an image of the Archangels Gabriel and Michael.

Tommy called to tell me that our cousin Wayland had died the week before. It wasn't terribly sad news to me because there had been so little communication among the three of us over the past thirty or so years and the affections that were once strong had considerably diminished. The conversation began pleasantly, as most of our telephone conversations did. Eventually the chitchat turned to family history. Tommy was retelling a story about an attempted robbery that took place in our grandfather Haggard's grocery store before either of us were born.

Our grandfather, Will Haggard, was an ill-tempered man, a trait that he evidently passed on to his son, Floyd, though not so much to his four daughters. An oddly formal grocerman, he wore a three-piece business suit that, in photographs at least, seemed to soften his hard demeanor. He carried a pocket watch in his vest that was attached to a watch chain and a T bar. According to Tommy, the robber, who was black and probably drunk, was afraid of our grandfather and probably wished he had never started this shit. Will Haggard was a Klansman, as was his son, and he wasn't afraid of the robber and didn't back away from him. He probably went under the counter and brought out the billy club he kept there for just this kind of situation. The robber responded by pulling out a knife. But when the old man still showed no fear, the robber, who by now must have been about to lose control of his bowels, thrust his knife at our grandfather's belly. But the point of the knife blade struck the watch in Will Haggard's vest pocket and stuck in the watch's gold cover.

Nobody knows the rest of the story. If there is an ending of some sort, neither Tommy nor I remembered it.

When he finished telling the story, I chuckled and said,

"You know, Tommy, it's funny how we remember the same story with different details. You know damned well that we heard it told by the same storyteller. You know, like out on Velma's porch after churning ice cream on a summer evening. And what's funny is that I don't remember that it was a black guy who stabbed old man Haggard, but a white guy who shot him and the *bullet* hit the pocket watch."

Tommy's response was immediate and terse.

"We still call 'em niggers down here."

There was a long pause as that word echoed in my head. He had done it again. I was trying to control my anger. Then I said, quietly,

"Well, I don't."

"I know you don't. Hell, you probably think it's OK that we give 'em all we give 'em, too, dontcha?"

"If we keep this up, Tommy, I'm gonna get mighty pissed off."

"So will I, just in the other direction."

"Fuck you . . . and don't bother ever calling me again until you can act like an adult human being."

I slammed the phone down.

I was shaking all over, weeping deeply, wondering what it would have been like to have grown up—and old—with a brother who allowed some room for my perspective. I couldn't work anymore because my hands were shaking. I couldn't eat either, so I went to my bedroom and tried to sleep.

The next morning I got up at five. I cleaned out the drawers in the bathroom cabinets. I made coffee. I fed my dogs. I did the morning chores.

And then I sat down to write my brother a letter. A letter incorporating as succinctly as I possibly could what I had been thinking about all through my sleepless night and my anxious morning. This is the text of that letter:

143

Tommy—

I am very sorry for the way our conversation ended yesterday. I really didn't mean to say that you shouldn't call me unless you could act like an adult human being. When I lose my composure my mind slips out of its usual fluency and I say dumb things like that.

No, what I really meant to say—what I really wish I had had the presence of mind to say at that very moment—was that you shouldn't call me until you can act like something other than an ignorant fucking redneck.

I have spent the better part of thirty-five years—in my classrooms and in my work—combating your brand of blind and stupid prejudice, your simpleminded and ignorant bigotry, and your arrogant and malignant notions of white superiority and supremacy. It saddens me beyond anything you can imagine that you, my brother, are the purebred and banal embodiment of all the things I hate.

Over the years I have tolerated your racial slurs in every conversation we have had, painful to me as they have been. I have suffered your insensitive slurs about women, too, especially painful since I am the father of three women whom I adore and the grandfather of five little girls. ("You know why they spank babies when they're born? So they'll knock the dicks off the dumb ones.") And I have endured your arrogant airs of superiority about matters that (as you confessed to me) you know nothing about—especially national and international politics. I have not called you to account for these things as I would have anybody else. I should have, because every time I have looked the other way, every time I have turned the other cheek, every time I have kept my mouth shut, my innate humanity has been diminished. And so has yours, though you don't know it.

And you are wrong that "we still call them niggers down here." I am still a southerner myself despite my place of residence—and if you don't understand that you do not understand what it means to be a true southerner. I travel throughout the South (far more than you, even though you live there) teaching and lecturing at places like Clemson and the Universities of Georgia, Mississippi, Tennessee, Texas, Oklahoma, and the like. I am close friends with many of the finest southern writers, educators, and journalists. And I can tell you that educated and cultured people in the South most assuredly do not think the way you think and do not call *them* niggers. Fortunately they, and not you and your ilk, are the ones who are molding the future of the American South.

The only people today who do think and speak the way you think and speak (in the South and elsewhere) are the ones who, like you, are full of hate, fear, and anger. And, curiously, they also seem to be the ones who, like you, speak inarticulately, slur their words, and are utterly incapable of correctly conjugating verbs. Their/your positions are not only intellectually indefensible, they are morally corrupt and contribute to the perpetuation of the greatest sickness of our age—racism.

You are an embarrassment to me, Tommy. You are an embarrassment because of your sadly comic sense of superiority and your outrageously bigoted attitudes. But mostly because of your persistent, rabid, and unapologetic racism. I am hurt and diminished by these things every time we talk and I do not wish to endure it ever again. I am ashamed that I am kin to you and will continue to be ashamed of our kinship as long as you harbor these perverted values and persist in rubbing my nose in them as you have done all my life. If you only knew how much pain you have inflicted on me over the past fifty years or so you couldn't help but be ashamed. If you can ever see the world from a slightly broader perspective than middle Tennessee, then perhaps we can salvage something of value from a brotherhood that has never amounted to very much—the saddest fact of my life.

Barry
December 3, 1997

TWO

FOUR MONTHS LATER, in April 1998, I was in Redlands, California, giving a talk at a conference of elementary school teachers. The talk had not gone well. It was the wrong speech for the wrong audience. The person who introduced me said (without querying me beforehand) that my presentation was going to be "fun." It was not. As soon as I was free of my obligations I walked back to the B&B where I was staying. I was down in the mouth because the morning had not gone well, so I lay down on the bed, thinking about my ineffectual speech. I picked up the phone and called home. When Cara, my oldest daughter, answered the phone, I asked her if there were any problems that needed my attention. She said,

"No. But you have a letter here from your brother."

I sat up and asked her if it was a thin envelope or a fat one.

"A fat one."

I bunched up a couple of pillows, lay back against them, and asked her to read the letter to me. What follows is the letter my brother wrote to me.

(For the record, I do not remember a Mary at the Country Club, nor a Johnnie B. Tommy always had a better memory for names than I have. I do remember Jimmy, the bartender. I have no idea who Nobie or Delores are or were, and neither do Tommy's sons. Why he brings up our cousin Helen Haggard as he does is not at all clear to me. He mentions watching *Huckleberry Finn* and is referencing a 1985 PBS film.)

Barry,

I am going to answer your question without any bullshit. I am going to save the first question for last. But first I want you to think, use that head of yours for something other than drawing pictures and writing letters showing off your intellectual wizardry.

Frankly the tone of your first letter has made me wonder if you deserve this letter. I too have not gone a day without thinking of you and you must believe that what I am about to tell you is the truth. At this late stage of our lives the air must be cleared.

First, don't believe anything Helen might tell you. In all our younger years, I can never remember seeing Helen on more than three or four occasions. She was never there. She doesn't have an opinion. If my memory serves me I think she failed to show up at Floyd's funeral. I could be wrong.

Helen like you left your roots of Shallowford Road. Hers at an early age. Teens I think. She literally fucked her way through the ranks of the Navy until she married Merle then dumped him for her present husband. The only reason she has contact with you is because of your esteem and stature.

Second: Wayland was a liar and a cheat. Maybe he will or has made it through the pearly gates, if so it was because he did take care of Bettye in her last years and days. I give him credit and respect for that.

When Velma died she had approximately $15,000.00 in a checking account and her will stated that money was to be split equally between you, Wayland, and myself. When I asked Wayland about the money he said that he and Bettye were on the signature for that account and that Velma said when she died all that money was to go to them because they took care of her. Bullshit!

Also to address that will: Bob gave the *Scamp* and Studebaker to me not Velma but when the boat was sold (to a guy named Earhardt) she took the money. When I traded the car for the '54 Ford blue convertible, Velma refused to sign the title over to me until I paid her some money. I don't remember how much. And she *never* put *any* money in an account for me much less $500.00 for an airline ticket. In 1962 you could fly anywhere in the U.S. for $60.00. Velma was a vicious bitch and very selfish. In her later years I had very little to do with [her] because of the way she treated Mother and Annie Lee. Bobbie is convinced to this day that my arthritis is pay back for the way I made fun of her and her pain. It's worth it! (What happened to the two bronze statues, the clocks, and the cook books? I thought you had them?)

Use some common sense about Bob. I loved him very much—he was like a second dad. But when Arthur died I stayed with Bob and Velma, you with Grandmother and that evil witch Minnie, they were partial to you. Big deal, forget it. Also Barry, you were different than any of us, Bob, Dad, and myself. I liked to hunt, fish, play ball, while you were more interested in your art and books. You even eluded [*sic*], to this in your *A Family Letter*. Your statement was "Industry and manliness are premium to this family which respects gun collections more than libraries, and measured a man by his business acumen and his ability to play football." Again big fucking deal. If we were all alike we would be boring and quite honestly sometimes I find you very boring simply because we don't have the same interests.

Now I want to get to the important stuff. My God I am so sorry for what you must have gone through as a child at my hands being bullied and all but honestly afterward I always felt bad. I remember once I pushed you down in front of Jimmy Livingood's house and you cut your leg bad and was bleeding. It scared the shit out of me. When mother put you in the tub it made the bleeding worse. I can hear you to this day saying "I'm going fast, I'm going fast."

When we became teens I wanted to whip your ass because you were so goddamn lazy. You would never help do anything, cut grass, paint, take out clinkers, stoke the furnace, nothing.

Barry this is the honest to God truth. When I was in the sixth grade and from that time on I never asked Mother or Dad for a dime. I worked cutting grass and painting wicker furniture with the spray painter I bought. Later working in service stations and foundries. I worked all my life, hard! When you were at Auburn where do you think your money came from? Mother and Dad didn't have it. I'm the one who put money in your checking account, not a lot but some. You even called me from Auburn one Sunday afternoon (I was fucking Anna Sue at the time). I told you that Mom and Dad were not at home and you said [that you] just wanted to talk to [me] not them. After our conversation I went outside and cried. I missed you so much.

Now I want to tell you about pain as a child. When I was three and Minnie was keeping us she would lock me in that dark pantry off the kitchen with no window, those high shelves and that trap door in the floor. She would leave me there for hours and stand outside making weird sounds. She would whip me unmercifully. In today's society she would be in prison. *Maybe* I took that out on you later. I never forgot those days and nights in that pantry. I was eighteen or so before I could sleep in a room without a light. I'll trade you a little taste of blood for that.

Charlie Chaplin said, "A day without laughter is a day wasted." The blacks and women are just subjects of humor, just like my crossed eye. I don't hate blacks but I do hate affirmative action, racial preference, and equal opportunities. We have been forced in this great country of ours to accept the black man as a race rather than an individual. These feelings I have now are not the same feelings I had twenty years ago and has nothing to do with the way we were brought up. When we lived at the Country Club did the blacks not like me the same as you? I know they did, if not better. I ate in the kitchen with them, laughed with them, and always treated them with respect. Mary sent me brownies when I was at Fort Sill, Johnny B. wrote me letters. Jimmy drove me to the bus station when I went in the Army. I have black friends, I could give you names and numbers. These people feel no prejudice from me. I sent money to Nobie when her son was in an auto accident; I sent airline tickets to Delores to go to California to see her dying brother. The color of their skins never come to mind. They were people that love and feel the same as me.

I, like you, do not want to have a conversation with you at this time. Your next letter, if any, will determine that. But I want to set you straight about one thing. I had to put up with the humiliation of being called stupid and ignorant at Baylor.

I may speak inarticulately, slur my words, and incorrectly conjugate verbs, but by God I can read my personal financial statement which makes me superior than most. I had served as president of the Chamber of Commerce, Mortgage Bankers Association and the Rotary Club having received the Paul Harris fellowship for outstanding service. Not bad for an ignorant fucking redneck. I am also fairly well read. I've read Dante, I prefer L'Amour. I've eaten caviar, I prefer peanut butter and I've listened to Chopin, I prefer Jimmy Buffet.

Barry, I know everything about you and you know *nothing* about me. I proudly display your works in my home and office, tears filled my eyes when you were on the Today Show. I watched all of *Huckleberry Finn* just to see your name in the credits at the end. I have framed the articles that were in *People Magazine* and *Newsweek* and *American Artist*. I do love you.

Just,

Tom

P.S. Don't grade this letter.

THREE

MOST OF THE PEOPLE I mention in my response to Tommy's letter you already know. You have not met Bernard Bagwell yet. Bernard was Wayland's half-brother. He was born blind. Bernard's wife, who was also blind, was Mary. When Bernard graduated from the Tennessee School for the Blind in Nashville, he and a friend, with less than five dollars between them, hitchhiked to California and back. He was a gifted singer and musician and made his living as a piano technician and as a soloist in churches and cathedrals in Memphis and Chicago. Jeanne is Jeanne Holmes Shepherd, Daddy's daughter. Hitt is James Hitt, one of my teachers at Baylor. The *Scamp* was our uncle Bob's very fast, red, white, and blue speedboat.

Dear Tommy,
Your letter came last Friday while I was in California. Cara called and told me that it had arrived. I asked her to open it and read it to me, which she did. I had her transcribe it and enter it into my journal.

Tommy, I can't help but grade your letter.

I give you an A. A good solid A.

You write well and you should do more of it.

And, my dear brother, you weren't the only one who was humiliated and made to feel stupid and second-class at Baylor. Do you think I escaped all that horseshit? Let me read you something I said in the speech I gave in California the morning I got your letter:

More than once I got into trouble at school for drawing naked women. One time was in the tenth grade. I was in a military school in Chattanooga. First Year Spanish. Winter term. Second period. Rain. The instructor was Señor Bazan. As usual, I was not paying attention to the lesson. Instead I was locked within my own mind, listening to the rain, and contemplating the roundness of breasts as I drew them on a blank page of my textbook. I didn't see him approaching. When he saw what I was doing he snapped me up by my shirt collar like a dog and made me leave the class and go report to the commandant, who made me empty my back pockets, bend over, and grab my ankles, whereupon he took his "board of education" to my backside. But, alas, the lesson didn't stick. I still draw naked figures.

And this from the same speech:

[Leonard] Baskin's influence . . . took root in a new-found intellectual life—something I had always wanted but felt incapable of since I didn't read much and since all through Baylor I was told, repeatedly, to keep my mouth shut and let people think I was a fool rather than open it and remove all doubt.

Tommy, I was called a moron, an imbecile, and an idiot. I was called slow and dim-witted. Hitt told me often that I was devoid of any intellectual curiosity and that I should never try to match wits with him because I only had half a wit.

I imagine that the only reason I have less feelings of anger and bitterness about Baylor than you do is because I was effectively asleep during my days there. Then again perhaps I was just slow and didn't realize what was happening to me and what was going on around me. Today I recognize it for what it was—we, you and I and others like us, were bullied by little men who aspired to greater things than they were capable of. I have taught in private schools for thirty years, Tommy, and I know these people well. They get stuck in a velvet trap and can't get out and then they vent their frustrations on their students. Damn them!

You are not stupid, Tommy. Never have been. No more than I am.

Your letter was not only well written and thoughtful, it was entertaining, humorous, and surprisingly lacking in anger. Not everybody can pull all that off in the same letter—especially when responding to a letter as vicious as my first one to you was. If you had written me the letter I wrote to you I would have been angry and vitriolic. I would certainly have been less graceful than you in my response.

You should try your hand at writing other things, Tommy—but if not, letters are fine. Just write them to me. Write me and tell me more about our growing up together because we certainly have different perceptions of that and that is the dirty linen we need to wash together and hang out to dry before one of us dies and the rift becomes eternal. Hearing your voice through your letter was a wonderful experience for me because I was able to go back and read a passage again, and to think on it, and to think about what I might say in response rather than just responding emotionally from my gut as I did on the phone last fall. And gut is the right word. I thought I was going to puke that afternoon.

Along this same line let me remind you of something, and this is something that you can go back and reread in my first letter and confirm for yourself. I did not say that you were an ignorant fucking redneck, I said that you "shouldn't call me until you can act like something other than an ignorant fucking redneck." "Act like" is the operative phrase there. And it is that "acting like" that causes me the pain and the embarrassment I spoke of. You got through seven pages of prose without ever using the word "nigger."

Do you realize that you have never done that with me in a conversation?

What am I to make of that if not that you do it, like my "big Ike" brother from childhood, just to piss me off? I hate that, and I don't want you to do it anymore. It hurts because, as I said to you, it diminishes me to hear you say things like that and to then hear my silence. You are welcome to your politics. Just don't rub my nose in them when you know full well that I think they suck. I have never done that to you, and I expect the same respect and consideration from you in return. I think that you have "acted" a lot throughout our lives together. Your good letter suggests that you are not as full of as much anger and spleen as you act like you are.

So let's talk about that letter now.

In your letter to me you say that "Frankly the tone of your first letter has made me wonder if you deserve this letter." You are right. As I have already admitted, the tone of my first letter was "viscious." It was written in anger and frustration. Angry at you for rubbing my nose in that racist horseshit that I hate so much, and frustrated with myself because I don't stand up to you when you do it. Abraham Lincoln said that a man keeping silent when he should speak makes that man a coward. I've been a coward with you for the sake of decorum since we speak so rarely and I ain't going to do it any more. So understand the reason for my tone and try to forgive me for it. Try to imagine that you held some very sacred ideals and ideas and that every time we talked I belittled those ideals and ideas. That will explain my tone.

And speaking of that, what ideals do you hold sacred, Tommy? Love? Devotion? Piety? That is not a rhetorical question. I really want to know. Not that I plan on belittling them if you are willing to wrestle them into words for me. To the contrary. I would like, before one of us dies, to have a conversation with you about ideas and ideals. About the things we hold dear. Sacred things. To share these things with each other without the fear of being mocked or scorned because the other one does not share the same feelings. I would like, finally, Tommy, to know who you are, because as you quite rightly say, I know nothing about you. By the same token, though, you only *think* that you know "everything" about me. You don't.

You speak of Helen as if you knew her. Again, you don't. And neither do I. I take what she says to me with no more, nor no less, seriousness than I take what anybody else says to me, even perfect strangers. I am sure that you would offer the same advice to me about Jeanne Holmes, too. But both of these people have interesting things to say. Interesting perceptions of past history. Those perceptions, like yours and mine, may be flawed. Then again, they may be right on the money. I just try to listen and then separate the wheat from the chaff. And separating those two things cannot be done without bringing to the task, once again, our own perceptions and prejudices. For instance, neither you nor I want to think of Mother as a selfish bitch. But—what if it is true that, as Jeanne says, Mother simply did not want Daddy to bring her to live with us? That it was neither Daddy's idea nor his mother's as we have been given to believe. It makes sense if you remember the story that Mother herself told about not wanting to be pregnant with me. Hell, she had the good life, didn't she? Rich husband. One kid. Maids. Why the hell would she want to fuck it up with another kid to have to take care of—especially after the money was gone, and even more especially if the kid wasn't her own? Anyway, it's all a matter of perception, isn't it? All our personal histories are remembered and retold through the filter and prism of perception. What you and I need to do is to compare our individual filters . . . to talk and to share with each other without ridiculing the things we each hold dear.

I found what you said about Velma,

the *Scamp,* and the Fort Sill money most interesting. Here again, you see, perception is at work. Along, in this case apparently, with some deception. I did not make up the story. Believe me. Velma told me that she had given you the money to come home if you got a furlough. I have a vague memory of overhearing her telling somebody about it in her living room. Maybe that's the case. Maybe I overheard it. Either way, she lied about it. I wonder why? She also told me that she gave you the car and the boat. You can imagine how it hurt then, four years later—me with two babies and unable to pay my bills—when I asked her if I could borrow fifty dollars for groceries and she said, hesitantly, "Yes, but you'll have to pay me back." How it hurt to get Bob's suitcase and table saw and you get a car and boat. If I had known that she had not favored you with the five hundred dollars, that it was Bob who gave you the *Scamp* and the Studebaker, I might not have felt so hurt. I don't know what became of the clock and the statuettes, Tommy. I seem to remember Velma telling me that there was a break-in and that they were stolen, but I don't know that for sure. She might have given them to that old fart that had the upholstery shop next door. I do know that she wouldn't let me take the woodworking equipment out of her basement even though she said that she had given it all to me, said that Bob wanted me to have it. And I think, if I remember this correctly, that she ended up giving it all to him. What was his name? You're so good at remembering details like that, whereas I am completely unable to.

You are right about my being different from everybody else, though I never perceived (there's that word again) of it that way. And you're right about my being lazy. Both of those things haunt me to this day.

Okay, I was different, but why was I different?

That was the central question in my last letter. Why, Tommy, were we (are we?) so different? We sucked the same sugar tits. We drank the same water, breathed the same air, listened to the same fucking chickens cluck and crow in the morning, everything the same, except food. At least as far as I can remember. And you are right—"Big fucking deal, if we were all alike we would be boring." I am not looking for homogenization here. I don't give a fuck if we are different, I just want to know what the factors are that precipitate the differences—especially the ideological differences that stand between us. Keep the differences. I am not trying to convince you to my way of thinking. Never have. Never will. Just explain to me, if you can (and if you can't, OK, but tell me that you can't), why we are so different—or *are* we, really, after all? What is your perception of that? It haunts me, Tommy. I am proud of who I am. Of what I've done. But this one issue truly haunts me because I think it has everything to do with who I am and what I have done and I don't understand it and I *want* to understand it.

Lazy? Yep, I was. Might even still be for that matter. I can still hear you calling me that. And Mother. And Bob. Floyd. Everybody. I keep a journal today. Have been for nearly twenty years, and the reason for keeping it isn't so much to keep a record of what I do (though that, too) as it is to have a document that I can go back to when I get to feeling like I've been a fat, lazy shit and that journal will verify the fact for me that I ain't. I work ten to twelve hours a day seven days a week fifty weeks out of the year and I still sometimes feel like I might be lazy. Afraid that some-body's gonna find me out. God help me! But even if I was lazy, it gave you no right of punishment, a right you *did* assume, an assumed right that you apparently thought granted you the freedom to whip me any-time you thought I needed to be whipped. So what if I didn't clean out the gutters? Cut the grass? Big fucking deal, eh? And if you remember, you wouldn't *let* me do anything in the yard. You were so fucking anal retentive you thought that anything I did would screw it up. Better I stay inside and help Mother with the laundry. How many times did you hang out the laundry, bro?

I sympathize greatly with your ordeal with Minnie Smith. And you are right—if she did that to you today she could be brought up on criminal charges. I can barely remember the woman today. I can't even conjure an image of what she looked like, not like I can Grandmother. Maybe they did show partiality to me. I was more like Arthur Boyd than you were—as we have been told so many times. Maybe that explains it. I don't know. Then again maybe they felt sorry for me because (as Wayland said to me when I visited him and Bettye) you were favored on

Shallowford Road because you were "the son none of [them] ever had." Those were Wayland's very words. I stuck in the "them" in that sentence in place of his word—"us." The difference between what you suffered at Minnie's hands and what I suffered at your hands was that you didn't live with her day in and day out. She was not a constant element of fear in your life like you were in mine. You could escape. I couldn't. And correct me on this part of the story if it's not correct (if it is, please don't feel like it's an indictment, because I am not after accusations here, I am after truth), but wasn't the primary reason she did that to you was because she was punishing you for mistreating your baby brother? If that is true, it does not make her crime any less. It just makes connections.

I have always admired your industriousness, Tommy. Your ability to work, to focus on something (a red MG convertible for instance) and go after it was admirable. Then and now. I had forgotten about the money you put into my checking account when I was at Auburn. I cried when I read that part of your letter (I cried at lots of parts, but I won't go into that—not now anyway). I just hope that you are not laboring under the delusion that you put me through school, or that you put more money into my account than Mother did. I may not have been as industrious as you when we were kids, but I did end up putting myself through college. As you remember I preached myself through the last two years. The salaries from Hixson Methodist Church and Newnan Springs Methodist Church and loans from the Methodist Church itself got me through. I didn't pay off the church loans until 1968. And I can read my financial statement too, Tommy, and it's pretty impressive, though not as much as yours is. But that does not make me superior to anybody, especially not most, and certainly not you.

Last week I spoke of you, as you have read, from a public podium with affection and good cheer. I have not always done so and you should know that. My past, especially my childhood, has become the source of a lot of my speeches and essay writing over the past few years. You know this because I've interviewed you for that purpose, like I interviewed Wayland and Bettye and Jeanne. I say this to preface my comments about my suffering your bullying. Here is one of the things I have written—you might want to take a break about now—go get a drink or something. It's about the bus.

At this point in my letter I recounted the story of our having been downtown to see a movie, our coming home on the public bus, my finding a seat in the back of the bus between two black women, and the repercussions of my doing so. Then I told him:

I don't have any more to say about bullying and whipping right now, Tom. I'd love to hear your response.

I was happy to hear of your good works and of the generosity and sensitivity you have extended to your black friends over the years. I was glad to hear that you indeed *have* black friends. And I'd be willing to wager that you don't use the word "nigger" in front of them—and that's one of the problems I have with you and that word, and why I think you use it mostly just to piss me off. I've got a big picture of your calling Michael Jordan a nigger to his face. Or Leontyne Price. Or Wole Soyinka. Tell me more about your black friends. Do you have them to your house? Do you take meals with them? Do you hug them when you see them after a long absence? And you see that's another problem I have with racism. As a visual artist I am completely dependent on my sight. So is racism, but in an entirely different way. Do you think that Bernard was a racist? Do you think that he could have possibly cared what color a man's skin is? I wanted to ask him this question. I asked Wayland if he thought that Bernard would entertain my coming to see him after not having talked with him in over thirty years. Wayland wasn't encouraging and I ended up waiting too long. When I did finally get up my gumption and called, Mary answered the phone and said that I couldn't talk with him because Bernard had died a few days before.

So please talk to me some more about this, Tommy. It's important to me.

And another thing. I can tell a politically incorrect joke as well as anybody. I have a lot of problems with being politically correct and don't think of myself as being so. I see it as so much soi-disant apologetics and a load of happy horseshit. I probably feel pretty much the same way you feel about affirmative action and racial preferences—though certainly not (as you said in your letter) about equal opportunities. By God, my daughters and granddaughters are going to have all the opportunities that your sons or anybody else's sons are to have or else I will die trying to make certain that they do. I simply cannot accept that one person has access to more opportunity than somebody else based on arbitrary and biased criteria like skin color, nationality, religion, or dicks. Fuck that shit. Imagine that sweet little granddaughter of yours being turned down someday for a job that she is perfectly capable of doing or being denied access to an educational or entertainment facility simply because she didn't have a tallywhacker hanging between her legs. Or because she had crossed eyes or freckles on her skin. Or only four fingers on a hand. Or was a Baptist. So when you tell me a joke about slapping babies on the butt to knock the dicks off the dumb ones, it rankles me because it offends my daughters—and your granddaughter. It offends my ex-wife. It offends a few women that I have slept with and been in love with. And it offends a whole lot of very close personal friends that don't have dicks who could chew you up and spit you out because they are so much smarter than you and me put together. But I told the joke to my daughters anyway. And they laughed.

This is a great country, Tommy, as you say. And it is great if for no other reason than it is a place where fair play is at least a possibility. Fair play to ALL people, regardless. No limitations. No exceptions. NO exceptions. That to me is a sacred notion—far more important than any religious precept I know of. And I can joke about any of it up to the point where I start to feel that it is no longer a joke. And your jokes sometimes leave me wondering. I need you to be clear about them with me.

And don't be too proud of your shit-kicker superiority about things cultural. I like peanut butter better than caviar, too. And since you've read your Dante (did you read the Mandelbaum translation, the one I illustrated back in the eighties?) you will understand me when I say that if we can continue this dialogue—in writing for a while longer, I hope—you and I, as brothers, may one day emerge from this morass, once again to see the stars—"*a riveder le stelle.*"

One final note: when I write to you it is not to show off any so-called intellectual "wizardry," as you accuse me of. I write to you in the same manner, using the same syntax and vocabulary, as I do when I write any close friend—I admit that I don't write business letters this way. I am not trying to impress you. I am not talking down to you, nor am I talking up to you. This is the way I think. This is my language. This is the way I write, like it or not. During the course of this correspondence I promise you that I will not question your language or correct your spelling. Do me the same courtesy because, if for no other reason, it just ain't that important.

There are probably things that I haven't said that I should have, but this has gone on long enough. Ask me questions.

I look forward to your next letter. Until then,

I am, like you,

Just,

Barry

April 24, 1998

Tommy and his horse, Red, c. 1980

• • •

THESE THREE LETTERS are all that there are. Tommy's one letter was written with a fountain pen in black ink on lined composition paper. His handwriting is a neat, well-paced, almost Victorian script. He crossed out very few words and made infrequent errors in spelling, punctuation, or grammar, proving me wrong about his being "inarticulate" and "utterly incapable of correctly conjugating verbs."

My letters were composed in my word processor on plain white paper. My spelling, punctuation, and usage were no better than his. It is unfortunate that these three letters are the whole of our exchange. For whatever reasons, we did not maintain the correspondence. I wish we had. I wish it had become habitual for both of us. Instead, we talked on the phone. We talked once or twice a month for the next seven years. We caught up on the lives of our children and grandchildren. We told jokes. Lots of them. (You know what PMS stands for? Pass my shotgun.) We swapped tales, both tall and real. We bitched and griped about getting old—it was a recurrent conversation and was always colored with humor. ("Making love at my age," Tommy once said, "is like trying to stuff a marshmallow into a parking meter.") We commiserated about the death of our dogs and about our own health and mortality—his cancer, my diabetes. Yet our conversations were never morbid or morose and they rarely ended without laughter and each saying to the other "I love you."

The first Friday of October 2002, I was in Nashville with my wife, Emily, to give a talk at the Nashville Public Library. As soon as we checked into our hotel room, I called Tommy and we made plans to have dinner that night at his place in Hendersonville. His son Todd was there with his wife, Tonya, and their two kids, Victoria and Olivia. Tyson was at the car races in Talledega that day, but his wife, Danielle, came. Nancy, my brother's new friend, was there, too, and she seemed to be good for Tommy. We spent several very enjoyable hours talking and telling old family stories.

On Sunday morning we met for brunch at the Union Station Hotel, where Emily and I were staying. Tommy was dressed well and groomed immaculately, as usual, looking like he might have been to church. I watched him at the buffet putting food on his plate that I never thought I'd see him eat, like pork sausage.

Over the meal Nancy told us about someone in her family, her daughter or her niece perhaps, who had adopted a black child, and that my brother had taken on the mantle of being that child's sponsor and protector. She told us that Tommy would go and pick him up and take him places and do things with him.

After brunch we went out to the hotel parking lot to say our good-byes. Tommy and I embraced, and as we did I kissed him on his cheek and said, "I love you." He hugged me even tighter and said, "I love you, too, my brother." Then he put his arms around Emily and hugged her for a long moment, too. Tommy genuinely liked Emily, and she him. Seeing them hold each other like that delighted my heart and melted what little ice that may have been lingering there.

A little before noon Emily and I got in our rented car, waved good-bye one last time, and drove to the airport. Two days later I wrote in my journal: "As the plane gained altitude I began to cry. And the tears come again as I write this: I love my brother. But now that we are here, in our late middle years, all the past ugliness seems to be a dream long ago dreamt. Either Tommy has changed, or I have, but more than likely both of us have. It was hard leaving him, especially as the plane climbed out of five thousand feet and I knew that somewhere in that autumn landscape beneath us, he and Nancy were out for a drive. And I know that the chances of our never seeing each other again alive will loom ever larger the older we get."

I never saw Tommy again. He died shortly after midnight on Tuesday, July 19, 2005. He was sixty-eight years old, six years younger than I am as I write this. A few years before his death, his bad eye became cancerous and was surgically removed. When Tommy called to tell me about the surgery and to report on his recovery, he seemed downright chipper about the whole thing. He made a joke about his new black eye patch. He thought that it complemented his bounteous white hair and made him look handsome and distinguished. He was right. It did.

His daughter-in-law Danielle called me at eight on that July morning with the news. She said that the cancer had metastasized and had attacked his kidneys, pancreas, spleen, and one of his ribs. She said that his heart gave out just trying to keep up. Whether there was any connection between that cancer and his childhood amblyopia I do not know, but it would seem unlikely if there were not.

During calling hours the evening before the funeral I sat at the far end of the funeral parlor, staying as far away from his body lying in that coffin as I could. Todd and Tyson came to me and asked if I wanted to see their Daddy. I did not. I could not. I wanted to remember him as he was the last time I saw him alive, before the cancer took his eye and gave him that eye patch he wore so proudly.

On the morning of the funeral, I sat with Tommy's sons and their families during the service and afterward accompanied them on the short and cheerless trip to the grave in Hendersonville Memory Gardens.

Though it wasn't far from the chapel, we took the funeral home limousine to the burial site. By the time we got there the casket was already on the lowering device and I watched an elderly man wipe away fingerprints on the polished coffin lid. I thought that Tommy would appreciate that simple gesture.

We sat in the shade of a blue canvas pavilion. The air was still and the late morning heat was beginning to tell, especially for those of us in black suits and black dresses. When the preacher finished saying the usual forgettable graveside words, the coffin was lowered into the ground. A few of us threw white carnations on it. When it was time for us to go, Tyson stood up, his eyes red from crying and his face puffed with grief. He took off his black jacket and handed it to Danielle. He picked up a shovel and attacked the pile of dry, ochre colored, stone-studded dirt. He attacked it as if *it* were to blame for his Daddy's death. He worked with frantic, almost hysterical dispatch. From where I stood he looked like a man not so much filling a grave hole, but a man trying to *save* a loved one who was buried alive.

After the ceremonies the family and friends gathered at Tommy's house for food, conversation, and reminiscences. Todd and Tyson were genial hosts and even managed a laugh or two at stories told about their Daddy. I stayed as long as I could, but I needed to get my borrowed car back to the friends who put Emily and me up. Emily had to leave earlier in the day, but I stayed over that night and flew home alone the next morning. It was a two-hour flight, so I had that time to sit back and think. To remember. To mourn. To weep. To be grateful that he did not die before we were able to reconcile. And to thank God for that little bit of grace.

TOMMY AND I ENJOYED eight years of brother-hood before he left, a brotherhood that was without anger, or recrimination, and without his ever again using the word *nigger* in conversation. That was eight years out of his allotted sixty-eight. Eight years out of my sixty-five. Not very much time for us to reconcile a discordant lifetime. But we did with it what we could. And when Tommy went on ahead, I hope that he left with peace in his heart. I know that the brother he left behind lives on with peace in *his* heart.

AFTERWORD

WILLIAM LOGAN, WRITING IN *Our Savage Art: Poetry and the Civil Tongue,* observed that "truth is the first victim of memoir." And that may well be the case. I know for certain that if my brother were alive, and if he were to read this, he would find many things to challenge. His memory of people's names, of places traveled to, and family legends and lore was always better than mine. And I am sure that he would put himself in a better light. I can say the same of my mother, my aunts, my uncles, my cousins, and all the characters in this story. Every one of them could make major and minor corrections and amendments. I cannot, and do not, claim that my memories are infallible or historically true. On the other hand, I can say that the stories I have told are true to the best of my recollections. True to my history as I recall it from a distant perspective. If I have looked back in error, or if I have forgotten the sequence of an event, or a date, or a person's name, or the exact location of an event, it is because the inexorable creep of time has rendered my memory old and imperfect, and I ask forgiveness if I have it wrong.

My childhood lingers in my memory like old movies filmed in a limited palette—dull ochres, deep umbers, with fleeting moments of rose madder—all framed by a peripheral gray-green fog. The kind of peripheral fog that frames my dreams, too. And I confess that many of my memories are influenced by photographs: the hue of the old pictures, the loss of focus of the faded ones, and the cracked emulsion and missing parts of the damaged ones.

By the same token, I suspect that some of my memories have been invented over the years around those pictures and that they are not, in fact, true historical memories. I do not know how to separate the invented from the remembered. But I do know that none of these stories are outright fiction.

Fiction does, however, play its part. The memories of my childhood abide in my mind like the bits and pieces of laundry that Mother and I hung on the backyard clothesline—a tiny pair of kid's skivvies here, a large chenille bedspread there—all held together by a line that is sometimes visible and other times not. They are like islands in an archipelago, as my friend the photographer Yola Monakhov has it. Each island is connected, under the surface, to the next, yet separated by water. Water that is sometimes bright and clear and other times dark and murky. I sometimes remember the beginning and the end of a story, but not the middle. I remember what happened, but not where—or when, exactly. So I have caulked the gaps in my memory with fictive elements.

Toward the end of the summer 2013, I wrote to my brother's sons. I said, "I am truly sorry that your Daddy ain't around to read this memoir. I'm rough on him here and there, but I'm rough on myself, too . . . but, hey, that's what a troubled brotherhood is about. I'm trying to tell the story as best I can. He and I had the best times the last few years he was alive. We buried our hatchets and enjoyed a few short years without an instance of anger or discord. In a way, this memoir is an homage to him as well as a history of our burdened brotherhood."

ACKNOWLEDGMENTS

Jeannie Braham, Paul Mariani, Bret Lott, Mira Bartok, Ann Patchett, and Tony Johnston for generously reading early drafts and parts of early drafts and offering helpful advice.

At the University of Tennessee at Chattanooga: Verbie Prevost, Steve Cox, Chapel Crowden, Kittrell Rushing, Hugh Prevost.

My good friend Charles Johnson.

Dr. Timothy Parsons for medical advice.

Todd Moser for photographing his great-grandfather's sword for me.

Tyson Moser for telling me stories about his daddy.

My brother, Tom; my step-sister Jeanne; my cousin Wayland, all of whom allowed me to interview them when the project was only an idea. They have all gone on ahead.

Mildred Rawlings, director of the Hedges Library at Baylor School and her colleagues Betsy Carmichael and Barbara Kennedy.

Karen Brown and her associates in the Local History and Genealogy Department of the Chattanooga Public Library.

Kathy Pories for making the story better than it was.

Craig Popelars for getting the first draft on Kathy Pories's desk.

And most of all to my beloved wife, Emily Crowe, for loving me, and for believing in me and this project. I love you, Miss Em, and this book is dedicated to you.

Parts of *Brothers* have previously appeared, in different forms, in the *Sewanee Review*, *Image Journal*, the *Oxford American*, the *Southern Review*, the *Ontario Review*, and *Parenthesis*.